Elite • 237

British Light Infantry in the American Revolution

ROBBIE MACNIVEN

ILLUSTRATED BY STEPHEN WALSH
Series editors Martin Windrow & Nick Reynolds

OSPREY PUBLISHING
Bloomsbury Publishing Plc
Kemp House, Chawley Park, Cumnor Hill, Oxford OX2 9PH, UK
1385 Broadway, 5th Floor, New York, NY 10018, USA
E-mail: info@ospreypublishing.com
www.ospreypublishing.com

OSPREY is a trademark of Osprey Publishing Ltd

First published in Great Britain in 2021

A catalog record for this book is available from the British Library.

ISBN: PB 9781472842497; eBook 9781472842503;
ePDF 9781472842473; XML 9781472842480

21 22 23 24 25   10 9 8 7 6 5 4 3 2 1

Edited by Nick Reynolds
Index by Rob Munro
Typeset by PDQ Digital Media Solutions, Bungay, UK
Printed and bound in India by Replika Press Private Ltd.

Osprey Publishing supports the Woodland Trust, the UK's leading woodland
conservation charity.

To find out more about our authors and books visit
www.ospreypublishing.com. Here you will find extracts, author
interviews, details of forthcoming events and the option to sign up for our
newsletter.

Artist's note

Readers may care to note that the original paintings from which the color
plates in this book were prepared are available for private sale. All
reproduction copyright whatsoever is retained by the publishers. All
inquiries should be addressed to:

walshillustrations@btinternet.com

The publishers regret that they can enter into no correspondence upon this
matter.

TITLE PAGE PHOTO: Lock detail on a reproduction musket. This includes
the doghead with its jaws and jaw screw, which held the flint in place. In
front of it was the pan and hammer (here capped by a leather slip that
would be removed in combat), along with the spring. Note the royal cipher
and the Tower inscription marking the weapon as property of the Board of
Ordnance and sourced from the Tower of London's armory. (Courtesy of the
4th Regiment of Foot)

CONTENTS

British Light Infantry in the American Revolution

INTRODUCTION

Starting in the mid-18th century, the British Army began to experiment with the use of light infantry, deploying them in companies and battalions to supplement British efforts across the globe during the Seven Years' War (1756–63). While the addition of light companies to regular battalions and the experimental creation of dedicated light-infantry regiments greatly benefited Britain's military campaigns, especially during the French and Indian War (1754–63) in North America, the new light troops did not continue in service after the war came to an end. The practice of having light companies in regular regiments was ended in 1763, and regiments which had specialized in light tactics were either disbanded or reverted to standard regulations. Despite this, British officers such as Lieutenant-Colonel William Howe and Major-General Thomas Gage, who had served in the light formations during the war, retained an interest in the potential of light infantry on the regular establishments.

Beginning in 1771, light-infantry companies were reintroduced into the line regiments of the British Army. Interest in just how the light infantry would function in future conflicts was exemplified by Howe when, in 1774, he formed a training camp for light troops at Salisbury, Wiltshire and demonstrated their abilities in front of King George III. The outbreak of the American Revolutionary War (1775–83) accelerated the reintroduction of light-infantry formations and doctrines into the British Army, manifesting itself in the operational brigading of light companies into composite battalions and practical Army-wide changes, such as the use of open-order tactics and modifications that made uniforms more practical for campaigning in North America. While initially ill-equipped to deal with the revolutionary movement in America, by mid-1776 British forces stood poised for the counterstrike that would reclaim New York for the Crown and nearly destroy General George Washington's recently formed Continental Army.

British light infantry, whether in companies or composite battalions, fought in every major battle and

A portrait of Captain Thomas Hewitt, 10th Regiment of Foot, 1781, by William Tate (1747–1806). Hewitt received his commission in 1772, becoming a lieutenant in 1775 and a captain in 1777. A year later he was given command of the 10th Foot's light-infantry company. His portrait gives a good indication of the uniform changes adopted by the light infantry, including the black belts, shoulder wings, red waistcoat, the small buttons used on the jacket, his light-infantry cap, and the short officer's fusil and bayonet. The red cord over the belt on his left shoulder is doubtless attached to a powder horn slung under his right arm. (Image courtesy of the National Army Museum, London)

many minor engagements during the American Revolution. Generally able to match rebel irregulars and militia in skirmishing and "Indian fighting," but also frequently called upon to act as crack shock troops in special operations, the so-called "Light Bobs" earned a reputation among both friends and foes as the ruthless elite of the British Army. Their success on the battlefield was mirrored not only by the light companies of the American Loyalist Provincial regiments, but also by the Continental Army, which established its own permanent light-infantry corps in 1777. By the time of the siege of Yorktown (September 28–October 19, 1781), the Continental Army's light-infantry regiments comprised an entire division.

Though the light infantry were highly active during the American Revolutionary War, many of the light-infantry lessons learned by the British Army were once again forgotten at the end of the conflict. British forces initially found themselves struggling to deal with the massed skirmishers deployed by Revolutionary France in the 1790s, and it would take the efforts of veterans of the American Revolutionary War, such as Lieutenant-General Sir John Moore, to champion light-infantry tactics in time for success against Napoleon.

ORIGINS

The basic concept of light infantry has existed for as long as recorded human conflict. By the early 18th century, however, the employment of regular light-infantry formations occurred only on the periphery of European conflict, most notably in the Habsburg Empire's wars with the Ottomans and the Russian Empire's use of steppe peoples such as the Cossacks. The success of the irregular light-infantry *Pandurs* under the Habsburg Monarchy during the War of the Austrian Succession (1740–48) was followed by the similar use of Croatian *Grenzers* during the Seven Years' War. Frederick the Great, King of Prussia, raised his own *Jäger* (hunters) for the Prussian Army. In 1743, Charles Louis Auguste Fouquet, duc de Belle-Isle and *Maréchal de France*, oversaw the creation of a mixed regiment of foot and horse in the French Army, to be known as *chasseurs*. Similarly, in 1760 Major Simon Fraser, a British officer who was serving as aide-de-camp to Prince Ferdinand of Brunswick during the Seven Years' War, assumed command of a regiment of volunteers drawn from the British battalions serving in Ferdinand's army. The composite force, known as "Fraser's Chasseurs," appears to have taken on a light-infantry role, and was commended for its effectiveness in an action against the French at Wezen on November 9, 1761.

While the European development of Britain's light-infantry concept in the 18th century has often been underappreciated, it is clear that it was the French and Indian War that had the greatest impact on the introduction of light-infantry formations and doctrines into the British Army. The standard warfare of the period was often incredibly difficult to conduct on Britain's colonial frontiers, a fact brought into sharp focus by the destruction of Major-General Edward Braddock's column by a small force of French and Native American irregulars close to the Monongahela River on July 9, 1755. At both the tactical and operational level, British soldiers and their leaders were required to adapt quickly to both an unconventional environment and an unconventional enemy.

Many British Army officers serving during the Seven Years' War had already experienced a form of irregular warfare on what a good number of them would have classed a frontier wilderness, namely the suppression of the 1745 Jacobite uprising in the highlands of Scotland. The pacification of northern Scotland after the battle of Culloden (April 16, 1746) not only gave the British Army's officer corps an early taste of the distinctive requirements of irregular fighting in hostile terrain, but also emphasized the potential of Highland soldiers in wilderness warfare. Indeed, it has been argued that the independent companies and the early Highland regiments in the British Army, such as the 43rd (later 42nd) Foot or the 87th and 88th Foot, constituted the first complete light-infantry units. While such an understanding is somewhat tenuous, it is clear that the experiences of Highland warfare – and indeed the appreciation of its difficulties among Scottish officers in the British Army, such as Lieutenant-Colonel John Forbes of the Scots Greys – played a role in preparing Britain's military for large-scale campaigning in North America's backwoods.

The British colonists in America had engaged in irregular warfare to combat both their Native American opponents and other colonists since the founding of Jamestown by English settlers in May 1607. Despite this, the expansion of Britain's imperial domains meant that the average colonial

ten button holes. ‖ - ‖.

16 by he.

red yellow white

Kings arms. in

Tyger Skinn.

Rutland

Sketch of a Glamorgan light infantryman by Philip James de Loutherbourg (1740–1812), c.1778. The Glamorgan Regiment was one of a number of militia regiments raised in 1778, following France's entry into the war on the side of the Patriots. While not regulars, the British militia were equipped in an almost identical fashion to the standing Army. (Anne S.K. Brown Military Collection, Brown University Library) militiaman in the 1750s had comparatively little experience fighting the king's enemies in the unsettled parts of the country. The men most suited to such a conflict were the frontier bands of scouts and rangers formed by British Army officers. These men, mostly Americans, included Captain Robert Rogers and Captain Israel Putnam of Rogers' Rangers, an independent ranger company. While such outfits proved their usefulness on a number of occasions, they were often viewed as ill-disciplined and unreliable by senior British Army officers. The Duke of Cumberland, corresponding with the British commander-in-chief in North America, Lord Loudoun, summed up the preference for regular soldiers being converted to fulfill the roles of colonial rangers when he wrote that "till Regular Officers with men that they can trust, learn to beat the woods, & act as Irregulars, you will never gain any certain Intelligence of the Enemy" (LO 2065).

In 1757 Loudoun authorized the creation of a "cadet corps" to be overseen by Rogers, geared toward training regular officers and volunteers in the art of wilderness warfare. Loudoun hoped that once such a corps had been established, its members could spread their newfound skills among soldiers of their old units. He also authorized Colonel Thomas Gage, an officer of the 44th Foot who had survived Braddock's disaster in 1755, to raise a dedicated regiment of light infantry from among the regiments in North America.

Styled the 80th Regiment of Light-Armed Foot, Gage's experiment was likely as much a vehicle for his own promotion as it was a desire to espouse the potential of new light-infantry tactics. Part of his pitch to Loudoun for the formation of the regiment involved the fact that rangers received greater pay than regular soldiers, and by reducing the need for rangers the military could thus reduce the amount it spent on them (in reality, however, the size of and reliance on the ranger corps continued to grow throughout the war, much to Gage's chagrin). A total of 100 soldiers from several regular regiments were drafted into the 80th, with most of the remaining recruits being provided by American colonists. Among the initial officers were men from the regulars who had spent time with Rogers' cadet corps, such as Thomas Drought and William Irwin of the 44th Foot, William Fraser from the 42nd Highlanders, and Nicholas Ward of the 62nd Foot (redesignated the 60th in February 1757).

The regiment's uniform was unique among the regular establishment, and emphasized the practical changes wrought by fighting on the frontier. Rather than red, the woolen regimental coat was dark brown in color, without lace and cut down to a tight fit with the tails removed. The men were initially clad in the same red beeches and waistcoats as other regiments, but later adopted brown for those articles of clothing as well, with black buttons for the entire ensemble. Cocked hats were replaced with small leather caps. Muskets were initially cut down and browned (a process that protected the weapon's metal components from rust), and then replaced with .66-caliber carbines, while short swords were swapped for tomahawks.

While it was the first example of a light-infantry regiment in the British Army, the 80th Light-Armed Foot was not the only light-infantry experiment conducted by Britain's "American army." Concurrent with the creation of the 80th were the efforts of George Augustus Howe, the young colonel of the 55th Foot, who sought to convert his regiment to the style of colonial rangers. Howe had served with Rogers in 1757 and assimilated much of the "bushfighting" for which the commander of Rogers' Rangers had

Sketch of the side and rear view of a Glamorgan militia light infantryman by Philip James de Loutherbourg, c.1778. Note the two cartridge boxes and bayonet, the powder horn, and a further pouch likely for loose balls and leather patches for the rifle. (Anne S.K. Brown Military Collection, Brown University Library)

become famous. He sought to emulate the rangers in much the same way as the 80th had, removing the coat tails from regimental uniforms, cutting down cocked hats, browning muskets, replacing gaiters with hardwearing leggings, and having his men crop their hair. While the changes didn't go so far as those instituted in Gage's regiment, the differences between the 55th and unmodified line regiments were still stark. Unlike Gage's experiment, however, Howe's (by now a brigadier general) was cut short by his death outside Fort Ticonderoga on July 6, 1758. His replacement, Brigadier-General John Prideaux, was likewise killed just over a year later, on July 17, 1759, at the battle of Fort Niagara, and henceforth the 55th was discontinued as a body of light infantry.

The 60th Foot was another unit involved in the early use of regimental-wide light-infantry doctrine. Originally raised in 1755 as the 62nd (Royal American) Regiment of Foot, the four battalions were intended to be formed from recruits drawn from the American colonists, partly to reduce the reliance on the colonial Provincial Corps, which was looked down upon by some British Army officers. Recruitment in America proved unfruitful, however, and most of the regiment's men ended up being drawn from Ireland and European Protestants who had settled in Britain.

With the 60th Foot having been conceived of from the beginning as a force designed to fight in the North American wilderness, the regimental uniform was devoid of lace, and its officers introduced modifications much like those applied to the 80th and 55th Foot. Two Swiss battalion commanders in particular, Lieutenant-Colonel Henry Bouquet and Lieutenant-Colonel Frederick Haldimand, championed a focus on light-infantry tactics. (The 60th eventually went on to become one of the first regiments in the British Army to be fully equipped with rifles.) Continuing the trend set by those already on campaign, authorization was given to raise a specifically trained light-infantry regiment, the 85th Regiment of Foot, in Britain in 1759 – it participated in the capture the island of Belle-Île off the French coast in June 1761, and a year later was deployed to Portugal, though how frequently the unit was actually utilized in light-infantry roles is debatable.

All of the regiments mentioned emphasized more than just cosmetic changes for the North American terrain. Light infantrymen were picked for a range of abilities that placed them apart from most 18th-century soldiers. They were to be extremely fit, able to cover large tracts of untamed land at pace, as well as being capable marksmen and possessed of initiative and the ability to act independently. Often characterized as ragamuffins and scoundrels, they nevertheless rapidly developed a strong sense of martial pride and a confidence in their own abilities. In 1759 Major-General James Wolfe's orders for the Quebec campaign encapsulated their versatility and their predatory spirit – "light infantry have no fixed post in the order of battle, they will be thrown upon one or other of the wings, with a view to take the enemy's flank, or rear if occasion offers" (quoted in Knox 1769: 55). Nor were regiments trained as light infantry the only ones to embrace the talents of such men. While various officers took the initiative when it came to outfitting and training their units as light troops, of equal importance was the introduction of dedicated light-infantry companies into the otherwise unmodified line regiments on the British and Irish Establishments and the subsequent creation of the provisional light battalions.

As part of the preparations for the British attack on Louisbourg (situated on Cape Breton Island, Nova Scotia) commencing in early June 1758, Major-General Jeffery Amherst ordered the formation of a light-infantry battalion, specifically "a Body of light troops … to oppose the Indians, Canadians, and other painted Savages" able to "entertain them in their own way"; volunteers from regiments newly arrived from Europe were to be chosen based on those who were "active marchers" and "experts at firing ball," while those who had already served in America would be considered if they were "good marksmen" and "most accustomed to the woods" (quoted in Gordon 1885: 107–08). In all 550 men were placed under the command of Major George Scott, and performed notable service during the successful Louisbourg expedition which set sail from Halifax, Nova Scotia, on May 29, 1758.

Disbanded in November 1758, the light infantrymen were again called upon for Wolfe's 1759 expedition to Quebec. This time, however, the lights were first formed as companies within their regular, parent regiments before being once again drawn together into a provisional light battalion, thus instigating the process that would be used to deploy light infantry during the American Revolutionary War. It is notable that the battalion's commander during the 1759 campaign was Lieutenant-Colonel William Howe, younger brother of George Howe and future commander-in-chief of British forces in North American. On the evening of September 12, 1759, Howe and his light infantry were the first men to scale the heights leading to the Plains of Abraham, outside Quebec, routing a French piquet in the process and paving the way for the rest of Wolfe's army to engage the enemy successfully the next day. Over the course of the one-day battle of the Plains of Abraham, Howe's light infantry also successfully shielded the left flank of Wolfe's line from the attentions of bands of enemy Native Americans and French-Canadian irregulars.

Over the course of the Seven Years' War the new light infantry proved to be an invaluable addition to Britain's military efforts, particularly in North America. Success came at a very literal cost, however. Victory over France and the acquisition of swathes of new territory left Britain with vast debts. As was so often the case, at the end of the war the size and strength of the British Army were immediately scaled back.

BRITISH LIGHT INFANTRY ON THE EVE OF THE AMERICAN REVOLUTIONARY WAR

The disbanding of the British Army's light companies and battalions by the end of 1764 was viewed as a cost-cutting exercise, but it was not approved of by all. Captain Bennett Cuthbertson, writing in 1768, claimed that the re-emergence of dedicated light-infantry companies would inevitably occur in a future conflict, and that they would prove to be invaluable not only as woodland skirmishers but as full battalions capable of being a driving force in any given campaign (Cuthbertson 1776: 190).

In 1771 the decision was taken to reintroduce light infantry, specifically in the form of a dedicated light company added to each of the 44 line regiments on the British Establishment. Each light company would consist, on paper, of one captain, two lieutenants, two sergeants, one drummer, three corporals, and 36 privates. This increased the number of companies in a regular British regiment from nine to ten, though the other companies were reduced in size to match that of the light company and keep the size of battalions the same. Each new light company would formally take post on the left of a battalion line in a mirror of the older grenadier companies that formed up on the right. The organizational efforts necessary to form such companies took place throughout the spring and summer of 1771. Uniforms and equipment were discussed and approved in March, with the records of commanding officers showing them placing orders for their men. For example, Lord Robert Bertie, colonel of the 7th Regiment of Foot, issued orders for accoutrements on June 22 and for caps on July 12, 1771, both presumably for his regiment's new company. Officers were granted commissions for the new tenth companies in the months that followed. Issuance records from the Tower of London also show said companies being equipped with muskets as early as February 1771.

Those regiments on the Irish Establishment followed the ones on the British Establishment within the same year. Unlike the British Establishment regiments, however, all officers on the Irish Establishment received their commissions on the same date:

Two re-enactors dressed as light infantrymen are here shown in marching order, with haversack and blanket roll. The one on the left represents a soldier of the 4th Regiment of Foot in about 1775, while the one on the right is uniformed and equipped as a soldier of the 40th Regiment of Foot during the 1777 Philadelphia campaign. On display are both a full knapsack and a blanket roll, as well as haversacks and canteens – a soldier's daily load. (Courtesy of the 4th Regiment of Foot)

September 1, 1771. The order directing that light companies be formed was written on September 18, 1771, and specified that the companies should be mustered on October 1. Arms were issued from Dublin Castle throughout the summer of 1772 (which has led to the erroneous belief among some sources that the Irish Establishment light companies were not actually formed until 1772).

The raising of the Irish Establishment light companies received further instruction in the form of the treatises of the Lord Lieutenant of Ireland, Lieutenant-General George Townshend. A Seven Years' War veteran, Townshend had fought with Wolfe outside Quebec in 1759, taking command after Wolfe's death on September 13. He was at the battle of Villinghausen (July 15–16, 1761) and was with the British expedition that resisted the invasion of Portugal in 1762 – a force which included a nominal dedicated light-infantry regiment, the 85th Foot.

A recreated light infantryman of the 4th Regiment of Foot as he would have appeared in 1775. This left-side view shows the haversack, tin canteen, and bayonet in its scabbard. Note the white belts, rather than black, a feature adopted by some light-infantry companies. Note also the "wings" worn by both light and grenadier companies to differentiate them from the regular "hatman" companies. The exact style varied from regiment to regiment. (Courtesy of the 4th Regiment of Foot)

Townshend's *Rules and Orders*

In May 1772, as the light companies in Ireland were still being equipped, Townshend issued his *Rules and Orders for the Discipline of the Light Infantry Companies in His Majesty's Army in Ireland*. The brief document addressed a range of topics, including how to handle arms in woodland terrain, how to maneuver in files, how to react in the event of an ambush, and the signaling of orders via "a loud whistle, a posting horn, or some other instrument capable of conveying a sufficient sound to be heard at a considerable Distance" (Townshend 1894: 549). Also covered was the importance of giving "irregular fire" as well as soldiers learning to "Cover themselves with Trees" and "large stones, broken Inclosures, old Houses, or any strong feature which presents itself upon the face of a Country" (Townshend 1894: 550). An emphasis was placed on skirmishing in file pairs, with one man covering his partner while he reloaded from cover. According to Townshend:

> Each file has an entire dependence upon itself … the Firelocks of the front and rear Men, are never to be unloaded at the same time. When the front Rank Man Fires, the Rear Rank Man is to make Ready and step up briskly before his Comrade, but is by no means to discharge his Firelock untill the other has loaded, and then he is to step briskly before the Rear Rank Man, and this method to be followed untill a signal shall be given for ceasing to Fire. This Mutual Defence and Confidence is one of the most Essential Principles of Light Infantry. (Townshend 1894: 549)

Townshend also dedicated time to the specifics of the light infantry's weapons, instructing how the men were to be "taught to fire at Marks, and each Soldier is to find out the proper Measure of Powder for his own Firelock and to make up his Cartridges accordingly," as well as pointing out that a light infantryman's "Existence may depend upon a Single Shot's taking place"; similarly, he stressed "each man must have a sufficient Number of Cartridges made up, But as it may be necessary to have recourse to the [powder] Horn, The Men are to be taught to load from it. Every part of the Accoutrements must be kept in Constant repair, the Tomahawks Sharp, and fit for Use" (Townshend 1894: 551).

Ultimately, Townshend's writings were clearly based on his experiences of the Seven Years' War and emphasized the thinking typical of commanders of that period – "the success of any Engagement in a Wood or Strong Country depends upon the Coolness and presence of Mind of the Commanding Officer, and the Silence and Obedience of the Men fully as much as upon their Bravery" (Townshend 1894: 550).

Howe's *Discipline*

Two years later, William Howe supplemented Townshend's manual with one of his own. *Discipline established by Major General Howe for Light Infantry in Battalion, Sarum September 1774* was, like Townshend's *Rules and Orders*, a far-from-comprehensive attempt at codifying British light-infantry doctrine in its entirety, but it does provide us with an insight into how he viewed light infantry, and how he intended to use them.

The manual was written as part of a light-infantry training exercise Howe organized at Salisbury over a period of six weeks in August and September 1774. The light companies from seven regular regiments were put through a series of drills personally conceived of by Howe. There was a particular focus on maneuvering, especially as a single battalion. Clearly Howe, likely recalling his experiences commanding a light-infantry battalion in 1759, hoped to employ his light troops as a composite force in the field.

Following the drilling at Salisbury a full review was held before King George III in Richmond Park on October 3. This did not consist simply of a demonstration of maneuvers but took the form of a mock battle across a variety of terrain, including woodland and a hill, and at one point incorporating a house. Furthermore, the light companies demonstrated that they were capable of fighting as regular line troops as well as skirmishers, conducting fire by platoon and by company and, near the end of the review, launching a frontal uphill charge against the "enemy." Here again we see Howe's later use of light infantry foreshadowed. During the American Revolution light companies, especially when brought together to form battalions, would be utilized as shock troops almost as frequently as skirmishers. It seems that Howe viewed the light infantry as a well-rounded elite that he hoped to entrust with multiple battlefield roles.

The activities at Salisbury and in Richmond Park did not lead to the creation of a comprehensive manual or single, standardized training regime for the British Army's light infantry. Given the fact that it only involved the companies from seven regiments, it is tempting to assume that the impact of the training exercise at Salisbury – held just six months before the outbreak of hostilities in America – was minimal. To do so, however, would be to put too much emphasis on written documentation alone. Just as it is certain that the light-infantry experiences of the Seven Years' War, though not fully codified, would have spread and remained broadly understood within the institution of the British Army following the conflict, so it can be assumed that the drills and exercises espoused by Howe would have also been understood and disseminated to some degree by those companies and officers involved. Corporal Roger Lamb of the 9th Foot recalled being "sent among several other non-commissioned officers to be instructed in the new exercise which shortly before had been introduced by His Majesty to be practised in the different regiments" (Lamb 1811: 89). He appears to have been part of what was essentially a training camp outside of Dublin in 1775 for what he described as "this excellent mode of discipline for light troops" (Lamb 1811: 89), where he was instructed in Howe's drill by soldiers of the 33rd Foot. While Lamb, writing decades after the event, may well have been conflating the specific instructions he was taught with a later light-infantry manual, it is worth pointing out that the 33rd was not one of the original regiments at Salisbury, and that the regiment's soldiers would likely have been shown Howe's drills by others. Similarly, Lamb himself did not belong to a dedicated light-infantry company.

The activities of one Major Christopher French add further evidence to the belief that light-infantry doctrine was being specifically taught and disseminated, at least among British forces in Ireland. A letter dated April 27, 1775 from Lord Rochford to Earl Harcourt, the Lord Lieutenant of Ireland answers the question as to whether French "should continue in Ireland to complete the disciplining of the light companies in that kingdom, or embark for New York with his corps" (quoted in Redington & Roberts 1899: 343); he was ultimately instructed to embark for New York. Clearly, the lack of hard documentary evidence about the specifics of new light-infantry drill is no reason to assume the thoughts of Howe and Townshend were not being spread and encouraged.

A recreated light infantrymen takes aim while prone. Lying flat was practiced in drills prior to the American Revolutionary War, and a number of accounts describe it being used during combat. (Courtesy of the 4th Regiment of Foot)

Indeed, the concept of dissemination through a diffusion of individuals was the exact same one that had been utilized in the early years of the Seven Years' War, when officers who took commissions in units such as the 80th Foot or the ranger cadet corps effectively promulgated light-infantry doctrine throughout the learning networks of the then American army. Such a spread of knowledge and ideas would be used again during the American Revolutionary War – when Howe oversaw open-order drills with his army at Halifax in 1776 one of the regiments present, the 47th Foot, was later deployed to Canada, where the unit taught Howe's concepts to those regiments already stationed there. It is even possible that Howe's *Discipline*, describing the Salisbury and Richmond Park maneuvers, may have been copied multiple times – the surviving document is numbered "287," perhaps implying that it was only one of many that could be spread throughout the British Army.

Training in Boston

Neither Townshend nor Howe's brief commentaries on British light infantry amounted to a comprehensive understanding of light-infantry doctrine within the British Army prior to the American Revolutionary War. On the eve of the first battles, however, it is clear that British commanders appreciated the potential of light infantry and were including them in the hard drilling that marked the buildup toward open hostility. A Scottish-born Virginian, Dr. Robert Honeyman, was visiting Boston in March 1775 when he observed British infantry conducting exercises on the town common, noting how while they received regular training they also had the ability to skirmish on the flanks, provide independent fire (including loading and firing while lying

The Mock Attack by Philip James de Loutherbourg, 1779. This piece features a mock battle fought during the military maneuvers at Warley in 1778. In the foreground of the image the lights of two companies are visible – the 69th and 6th regiments of Foot. The 69th personnel are shown moving forward in irregular order with arms trailed, under the directions of an officer. In front of them the 6th Foot lights are pushing on in support of a formed group of grenadiers, advancing in pairs and firing at will through broken terrain. While this provides a good example of the role of light troops as skirmishers, their opponents show how light infantry could form part of the main battle line. At right, the light company of the Glamorgan militia are formed into two ranks at close order alongside a trio of Royal Artillery cannon and a force of grenadiers. (Royal Collection Trust/© Her Majesty Queen Elizabeth II 2021) prone on the ground), and screen other bodies of troops as they formed and maneuvered (Honeyman 1939: 43–44).

Honeyman's account describes light infantry being utilized in their traditional roles as part of the British preparations under Lieutenant-General Thomas Gage. The former commander of the 80th Light-Armed Foot employed his light companies in skirmishing, irregular fire, and acting as both a vanguard and a rearguard. They also practiced with live ammunition, shooting at targets that included both replica human figures and moving marks placed in the water off the piers of Boston harbor. The use of musket balls added a further dimension to preparations – live firing was usually strictly regulated in peacetime, and regiments were typically allotted only a small amount of ammunition throughout the year for training purposes. The comparatively frequent use of powder and ball by the troops in Boston, combined with the complex exercises ordered by Gage on the town common, left little to the imagination concerning the impending conflict.

A

LIGHT-INFANTRY OFFICERS

(1) Major John Maitland, Marines, 2nd Battalion Light Infantry, 1776

John Maitland was born in 1734, the eighth son of the 6th Earl of Lauderdale. He served in the Marines during the Seven Years' War, losing his right arm in action. In 1774 he was elected as Member of Parliament for Haddington Burghs, and in 1775 raised to the rank of major in the Marines. In 1776 he was given command of the newly formed 2nd Battalion Light Infantry, along with Major Turner van Straubenzee of the 17th Regiment of Foot. Maitland is depicted here with a uniform newly modified along the lines of Howe's orders in 1776 – a fellow officer, Captain John Graves Simcoe, noted following the battle of Bunker Hill that he believed the high number of officers killed had been due to their distinctive uniforms, and added that changes had been made to make commissioned officers appear more like the enlisted men (Simcoe 1926: 47). Indeed, Maitland's fellow Marines major, John Pitcairn, was perhaps the most famous British casualty of the engagement near Bunker Hill.

Maitland commanded both the 2nd Battalion Light Infantry and his own Marine light-infantry companies in a number of operations, including the destruction of rebel shipping along the Delaware (May 8–9, 1778) and the attack at Old Tappan (September 27, 1778). Another Marines officer, Major Bald, singled out the Marine light infantry for particular praise, writing that "the two Light Companies run at the rebels like lions, and behaved most bravely" (quoted in Gillespie 1803: 229–30). In October 1778 Maitland transferred to the 1st Battalion of the 71st Regiment of Foot and served with distinction as a lieutenant colonel in Georgia and South Carolina. After force-marching a relief force through swamps to Savannah during the siege of September 16–October 18, 1779, he died on October 22 from malaria. In 1981 his remains were returned to his native Scotland and interred at St. Mary's Church in Haddington, East Lothian.

(2) Lieutenant Martin Hunter, 52nd Foot, 2nd Battalion Light Infantry, 1777

Born on September 7, 1757, Martin Hunter purchased a commission as an ensign in the 52nd Regiment of Foot in

1771. Raised to lieutenant in 1775, his regiment arrived in America in time for the opening engagements at Lexington and Concord (April 19, 1775). As a member of the light company he saw action on numerous occasions, including Bunker Hill (June 17, 1775), Brooklyn Heights (August 27, 1776), Brandywine (September 11, 1777), Fort Washington (November 16, 1776), and Germantown (October 4, 1777). During the battle of Paoli (September 20–21, 1777) he was wounded in his right hand; he wrote that he "kept up until I got faint with the loss of blood, and was obliged to sit down. A sergeant of the Company remained with me, and we should have been left behind had not [Lieutenant Richard] St. George missed me after the business was over, and immediately went to General Grey, who halted the detachment until I was found" (Hunter 1894: 31–32). Hunter is depicted here soon after being shot, wrapping his wounded hand with his officer's sash as he attempts to remain with his attacking company.

After the war Hunter was posted to India. By the time of his death on December 9, 1846, he was a full general and governor of Stirling Castle. He was also believed to be the last living survivor of Lexington and Concord.

(3) Lieutenant-Colonel Robert Abercromby, 37th Foot, Light Infantry Brigade commander, 1781

Born on October 21, 1740, Robert Abercromby was the younger brother of well-known Scottish soldier and politician Ralph Abercromby. A veteran of the Seven Years' War, Robert was commissioned as the lieutenant colonel of the 37th Regiment of Foot in 1773. In October 1776 he was given command of the 1st Battalion Light Infantry, following the injury of its commanding officer, Major Thomas Musgrave, during the engagement at Throg's Neck. He led the battalion throughout much of the war. By the siege of Yorktown (September 28–October 19, 1781) he was in command of the Light Infantry Brigade, which included the 1st and 2nd battalions. Following the war Abercrombie was posted to India, where he became the Governor of Bombay in 1793. He was elected Member of Parliament for the county of Clackmannan, Scotland, in 1798. He died at the age of 87 on November 3, 1827, the oldest general in the British Army.

WEAPONS, CLOTHING, AND EQUIPMENT

Outfitting and equipping the British Army in the 18th century involved a process that today might seem heavily decentralized. British soldiers were issued with equipment from a range of sources including their company commanding officer, their regiment's commanding officer, and the British government itself, and it is helpful to establish the terminology that was used to categorize weaponry, uniforms, and kit before describing the items individually.

Regimental Clothing: These objects were provided by each regiment's colonel to his men on an annual or multiyear basis and were paid for by the soldiers through stoppages during their first year of use. The term encompassed the regimental coat (shortened to a jacket by the light infantry), cloth vests or waistcoats, caps and hats, and cloth breeches.

Necessary Clothing: These items were typically provided by the regiment on an as-needed basis. They usually consisted of linen shirts, worsted stockings, garters, neck stocks and stock clasps, foraging caps, shoes, soles, shoe buckles, and gaiters (in the case of the light infantry, always half-gaiters). Breeches and gaiters were at times replaced by trousers of wool or linen depending on the season, and what soldiers called leggings – essentially long woolen gaiters.

Accoutrements: These were again provided by the regiment's colonel and remained his property. Accoutrements included: a cartridge pouch with sling, a powder horn and belt, a hatchet plus frog and case, a musket sling, and the brush and picker necessary for musket maintenance.

Arms: These were weapons and pieces of equipment supplied directly by the British government, and remained Crown property. They consisted of the firelock (in the case of the light infantry, the 1769 Short Land Pattern musket), a bayonet and its scabbard and frog, a cartridge box, and a further nine-hole cartridge box with a belt.

A reproduction 1769 Short Land Pattern British Army musket, plus blanket roll. This weapon was the standard firearm used by British light-infantry companies during the American Revolutionary War. Blankets could be rolled up tightly and secured with a sling, and were sometimes used like knapsacks to store a soldier's personal items and food. (Courtesy of the 4th Regiment of Foot)

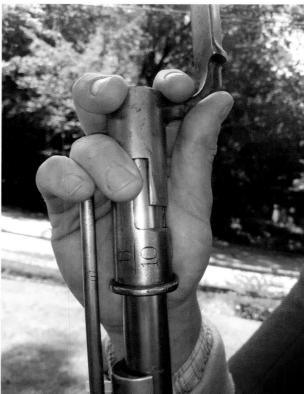

Ordinary Camp Necessaries: The final broad category of equipment, these items were, like the arms, Crown property, and included a tin water flask with string, a haversack, a knapsack, and a set of camp equipment (tin kettle with cover and bag, tent with poles, pins and mallet, and a hand hatchet for each five-man mess grouping).

While bearing in mind that equipping British soldiers was a varied business and definitions were diverse, the items described above have been categorized into weapons, uniforms, and equipment for ease of study.

Weapons

The smoothbore flintlock musket was the near-universal service firearm of all sides during the American Revolutionary War. A number of standardized flintlock patterns had been introduced in Britain earlier in the 18th century, most notably the .75-caliber Long Land Pattern and its eventual replacement, the .75-caliber Short Land Pattern. As the name suggests, the salient difference between the two designs was the barrel length, with the Short Land Pattern's 42in coming in at 4in less than the Long Land Pattern's 46in. During the American Revolutionary War the transition from Long to Short was still ongoing, and different regiments fought using different patterns, with occasional instances of both types even being used within the same regiment.

During the Seven Years' War British light infantry usually fought with either captured French muskets or 37in-barrel carbines. There remains some debate as to just which type of musket was issued to the re-formed light companies in 1771 and 1772. While it has been argued that they were provided with Pattern 1760 carbines, it seems that the weight of evidence points toward them actually being equipped with the new 1769 Short Land Pattern musket. Inspection returns, while not stating the pattern outright, describe new and different arms being issued to the light companies (Hagist & Goldstein 2009: 19–21).

Similarly, records for the issuing of ammunition during the American Revolutionary War show thousands of rounds being provided to the light-infantry battalions for muskets, and hundreds for the fusees employed by sergeants and officers, but no cartridge ammunition for carbines. Lastly, there are a number of original Pattern 1769 muskets of known provenance bearing light-infantry markings – LI, LC, or just L – still in existence, but almost no Pattern 1760 carbines with the appropriate engravings or stamps. On the balance of evidence it seems most likely that light infantrymen fought with Short Land Pattern muskets during the American Revolutionary War period, albeit with occasional exceptions – for example the Guards light infantry, like the rest of their regiment, continued to use the Long Land Pattern musket after the Short Land Pattern had replaced it in most other regiments, though there is evidence to suggest the Guards' lights eventually switched to the Short Land Pattern in 1780.

As mentioned, officers in the light companies were typically armed with fusils. These were either issued or purchased by the officers themselves, and were typically more expertly made, in a smaller caliber (usually .62), and with a slender stock and barrel. Contrary to popular belief, the barrels were not typically shorter than those of the Pattern 1769 muskets. There were some complaints that officers should not be focusing on loading and firing when they should be leading and addressing orders to their men during action, but it seems safe to assume that light-infantry officers, engaged as they were on more active service, would have had better recourse to the weapon than most. They also helped to make British officers appear more like their enlisted men, thus removing potential targets from the sights of enemy sharpshooters.

Turning to edged weapons, British light infantry were issued with bayonets in keeping with their Pattern 1769 muskets. The bayonets used a socket to attach to the musket's muzzle, with a long (usually between 12in and 17in), triangular blade of fluted steel. They were supplied with black leather scabbards with brass furniture and were kept on the waist belt, usually worn as a second crossbelt across the right shoulder. Officers also often carried bayonets for use with the fusee, though they tended to be shorter and more lightweight than those issued to enlisted men, as depicted in period portraiture.

Tomahawks had been formally added to the equipment of the British light infantry in 1759, aping the weapon's use among colonial frontiersmen and Native Americans. Usually referred to as hatchets or simply axes, they were typically carried in a buttoned case hung on the left side of the waist belt via a leather frog. The reinstituted light companies of 1771 continued to issue the weapon, albeit as an accoutrement issued by each regiment's colonel. Townshend's 1772 *Rules and Orders* stressed the importance of the weapon, stating that "the Hatchet Men of the Light Infantry Companies must be able Active Men and they should know how to Make Use of their Axes" (Townshend 1894: 551). Regardless of this, it seems likely that the tomahawk was most frequently employed as a campsite tool rather than a deadly weapon.

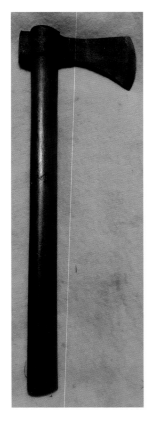
Reproduction hatchet. More of a tool than a weapon, this small axe was nevertheless another well-known piece of light-infantry equipment, born out of the use of tomahawks in the Seven Years' War. The new light companies were equipped with them from their first raising in 1771. (Courtesy of the 4th Regiment of Foot)

Mention should also be made of the rifled weapons employed by Britain's light infantry. While the importance of rifles used by some rebel forces during the American Revolutionary War has been somewhat overplayed in popular history, there is no doubt that the British took note of the deadly nature of the rifled weaponry employed against them early on in the war. The British government responded quickly to the threat, authorizing the creation of the British Army's first standard-issue service rifle in 1776.

During the Seven Years' War German-made rifles had been used by British Army soldiers, but the practice was far from widespread. The Pattern 1776 rifle – sometimes known as the "contract" rifle or Tower rifle – sought to rectify that. Initially, 200 were ordered from a Hanoverian gunmaker, August Heinrich Huhnstock, with the shipment used as the basis pattern for a further 800 supplied by four Birmingham gunsmiths – Mathias Barker & John Whately, Benjamin Willetts, William Grice, and Galton & Sons.

The Pattern 1776 rifle's original Hanoverian design was based on the typical German military rifles produced during the period. The barrel was 30.5in long with eight-groove rifling at .62 caliber. To make maintenance easy, the barrel was fitted with a break-off breech meaning it could easily be removed from its wooden stock and butt for cleaning purposes. It was also the first standardized British weapon to include a "captive" rammer, which operated on swivels held by a spring, thereby ensuring that the rammer wouldn't fly out of place during rough usage.

The new rifles were sent to America where they were issued to Crown forces, five to each light-dragoon troop and five to every company of light infantry, as well as to Loyalist Provincial regiments. It is likely the rifles saw heavy service – today there are only nine originals left – and they allowed British light infantry to compete on even terms with their enemies, with some Loyalist regiments such as the Queen's Rangers even equipping entire companies of riflemen.

As well as the Pattern 1776, another rifle entered British service early in the war thanks to the efforts of Major Patrick Ferguson. Designed by the

Original British Pattern 1776 "contract" rifle. In total, 1,000 of these weapons were produced and issued to British light infantrymen and dragoons in order to combat the threat of colonial riflemen. The sights (below) were more sophisticated for aiming than the bayonet lug featured on regular smoothbore flintlocks. (Photo courtesy of Morphy Auctions, www. morphyauctions.com)

Scottish officer, it was intended as a .65-caliber breech-loader that, ostensibly, could achieve a higher rate of fire than any traditional muzzle-loading gun. While its unusual design has made it far more famous than the "contract" rifles, the complaints that it was too fragile, too prone to fouling, and too expensive and complex to produce all appear to have been accurate, with the result that only 200 were ever made, of which just 100 saw active service, mostly serving with a rifle company specially equipped by Ferguson himself.

Clothing

In March 1771 a Board of General Officers was convened to decide how best to clothe and equip the new light-infantry companies (Strachan 1975: 187). On March 4 they provided a report on their recommendations, which received approval from King George III on March 22.

The creation of the new light companies took time, and regiments serving overseas appear to have undergone an interesting period of transition as they worked to keep up with the changes being authorized in Britain. The Minorca garrison, for example, initially styled the new light companies "piquet companies" in the case of the English regiments and a "highland company" in the case of the resident Scottish regiment. An image of one of these piquet-company privates in 1771 shows how the new uniform regulations were not immediately adopted in full. Orders for various pieces of light-infantry equipment appear periodically throughout 1771 and 1772, and variation continued to persist in practices such as headwear. In spite of this, a number of essential uniform elements were established as standard.

The most instantly recognizable component of the light-infantry uniform was the woolen regimental jacket, dyed madder red for the enlisted men and scarlet for the officers. It differed from the regimental coats of the

B LIGHT-INFANTRY WEAPONS, UNIFORMS, AND EQUIPMENT

(1) Private, 23rd Foot Light Company, 1776
The 23rd Foot, the Royal Welsh Fuzileers, was part of the initial expedition to Lexington and Concord in 1775 and fought in almost every major battle of the war. The 23rd Foot's light company was assigned to the 1st Battalion Light Infantry in 1776, becoming part of the 2nd Battalion in 1779. The exact style of cap worn by the 23rd Foot's light company is unknown – this design (and the one repeated on Plate C) is based on a similar depiction from 1780.

(2) Rifle-armed private, 40th Foot, 2nd Battalion Light Infantry, 1778
This private of the 40th Foot is equipped with one of the Pattern 1776 "contract" rifles, ordered by the British government in order to counter rifles used by the American colonists. Five were issued to every light company. Accurate at 300yd, they allowed Crown forces to fulfill skirmishing and harassment roles more effectively. As well as his regular equipment, he carries a separate pouch for loose balls and leather patches, the latter of which were wrapped around the balls to allow them to grip the rifled bore better and achieve a surer flight.

The 40th's light company was one of those deployed to St. Lucia, a French colony in the Caribbean, in an effort to repulse a full French invasion of the island in December 1778. They engaged French forces during the battle of the Vigie

Peninsula on December 18, helping to defeat three successive attacks on British positions.

(3) Private, 71st Foot Light Company, 1778
At first glance this private of the 71st Foot looks more like a dismounted dragoon than a light infantryman. The 71st was a Highland regiment which served with particular distinction in the southern colonies from 1778 onwards. Like the soldiers of all Highland regiments, the men of the 71st quickly replaced their kilts with legwear more suitable to the North American climate. During the siege of Savannah (September 16–October 18, 1779), 50 men were detached from the regiment's various companies to serve as dragoons. They were provided with dragoon uniforms, which were adjusted during the sea voyage from New York to Savannah. When this uniform style was combined with the design of light-infantry cap worn by the 71st – already very similar to the crested hats worn by Lieutenant-Colonel Banastre Tarleton's British Legion – the look was complete.

It should be noted that not all Highland regiments adopted caps for their light-infantry companies, or indeed bearskins for grenadiers. The returns of the 74th Foot, for example, list no caps or bearskins, only the standard bonnets worn by the regular companies, implying that all companies in the regiment wore them. Conversely, the 42nd Foot's clothing and shipping invoices show the number of bonnets to be short two companies, implying that the light infantry and grenadiers wore caps and bearskins respectively.

"hatman" companies in four salient particulars. First, it was cut down to short skirts, an aspect that led to it being accurately described as a jacket rather than a coat. While soldiers outside of the light companies regularly shortened their skirts when on campaign in North America, the light companies were the only ones to be issued shortened coats instead of cutting them down after issue. Second, light infantrymen sported sewn-on "wings" on their jacket shoulders, where the upper sleeve met the torso. These were considered the mark of an elite outfit responsible for protecting the flanks or "wings" and likewise featured on the shoulders of the grenadier companies. Third, while there is scant evidence to support it being general practice, period portraiture appears to show that at least some light-infantry officers used smaller buttons on their jackets. The regular companies tended to have small buttons on their waistcoats, with larger ones featuring on the cuffs and lapels of their regimental coats. In some paintings we see that the smaller buttons were used on both waistcoats and regimental jackets, though just how widespread this practice was is difficult to ascertain. Finally, the pocket flaps of the regimental jacket tended to be vertical rather than horizontal.

Beneath his jacket, the light infantryman wore a short, sleeveless, square-fronted waistcoat, red like the jacket (and unlike the white waistcoats of most regulars). The front was laced like the regimental jacket – another distinction from the unlaced waistcoats of the regulars – and the waistcoat was in turn worn over a white linen shirt, the loose collar of which was usually bound up by a simple black cloth stock or neckpiece tied or secured with clasps. During some campaigns, most notably in 1777 and later in the South, light companies left their regimental jackets in store and wore only their red waistcoats, sometimes unlaced, with sleeves sewn on.

25

Another distinctive element of the light-infantry uniform, at least initially, was the headwear. Most line-regiment soldiers wore cocked hats, with grenadiers and fusiliers sporting miters and, after the 1768 uniform-regulation changes, bearskins (though actually wearing such expensive and somewhat cumbersome pieces of headgear on campaign seems to have been a rarity). Indeed, the black cocked hat with its black cockade and white trim defined most British infantry to such a degree that the regular companies of line regiments were often termed the "hatman" companies. By contrast, the light infantry sported caps of leather or felt with stiff vertical front plates, often some type of visor, and other details such as feathers or crests that varied from regiment to regiment. These were clearly based on the practical leather caps adopted by some light-infantry units during the Seven Years' War, such as Gage's 80th, whose use of the caps was so ubiquitous that the regiment became known colloquially as the "leathercaps."

The British Army during the American Revolutionary War sported an at-times-bewildering array of legwear. Gaiters, specifically long ones reaching to the knee or mid-thigh and worn over breeches and stockings, were the standard garments for most British soldiers during the Seven Years' War period. Typically made from linen, twill, or woolen cloth, by the time of issuing of the new 1768 uniform warrant half-gaiters had also started to become popular. These half-gaiters were the standard issue for light infantry in 1771, but during the American Revolutionary War a third form of legwear became popular, known by the soldiers as trowsers, overalls or, more rarely, gaitered trowsers. Made from linen, wool, or cloth, they were in effect close-fitting trousers that tapered out to a gaitered bottom on each leg.

All light companies were initially issued with half-gaiters (this page) when first raised in the early 1770s. Gaiter-trousers (opposite) became increasingly popular among both light infantry and regular soldiers as the war progressed. Usually made with linen for summer wear, they were constructed from heavier cloth for winter months. (Courtesy of the 4th Regiment of Foot)

Equipment

To the light infantry's clothing was added kit that fell under both the "Accoutrements" and "Arms" categories. A black, tanned leather crossbelt was used to secure a cartridge pouch, while the waist belt, also black leather and bearing a plate inscribed with the regimental number or crest, kept the soldier's bayonet scabbard handy. Contrary to how it was worn in Britain, in North America most British soldiers took to wearing the waist belt as a second crossbelt over the right shoulder, with some modifying it to be permanently worn over the shoulder.

Ammunition was stored in a number of different ways, but the most frequently used was the cartridge pouch. Made of leather and usually adorned with a brass badge depicting the regimental crest or royal cipher, the pouch contained a block of wood drilled with holes for storing cartridges as well as small tools for musket maintenance and cartridge making (such as a tube for powder measuring) and was worn at the right hip attached to the end of the crossbelt slung over the left shoulder. The cartridge pouches used by the light infantry were typically lighter than those used by regular infantrymen.

Additional cartridges were stored in cartridge boxes, not to be confused with the cartridge pouch. The box was a wooden block drilled with holes for cartridges, similar to the one stored inside the cartridge pouch but covered by two leather flaps, one over the other, and attached to a leather strap worn around the waist, often alongside a leather frog for a bayonet scabbard. Soldiers of light-infantry companies were issued with two cartridge boxes, one for 18 cartridges and a smaller one for nine. In practice they proved unpopular, being prone to overturning easily and dumping all of the ammunition inside on the ground. Regiments tended to leave the cartridge boxes in storage during the American Revolutionary War, or wore them slung over the right shoulder.

Light infantry could also store spare cartridges wrapped in bladder skins in their knapsacks, and rifle-armed soldiers carried small pouches containing loose balls and leather patches for use in conjunction with the other source of ammunition – powder horns. These became popular during the Seven Years' War and were occasionally held on a Native American-style tumpline or, more typically, a simple cord that was itself attached to the crossbelt holding the cartridge pouch over the left shoulder. The horn's purpose was to hold finer-grain powder that supposedly provided greater accuracy. Like the cartridge box, the powder horn seems not to have been held in particularly

---

C | **LIGHT-INFANTRY CAPS**

Light-infantry caps could vary a great deal from regiment to regiment. Chosen by the regimental colonel, they were intended to be more lightweight and less disruptive for troops moving at speed or through forested terrain. Similar caps were prescribed for Major-General John Burgoyne's entire army for the 1777 Quebec campaign. Ultimately, however, they were judged to be uncomfortable and cumbersome (Strachan 1975: 192), and were largely phased out after the war. Here we see caps for six regiments of Foot: the 3rd (**1**), 5th (**2**), 10th (**3**), 23rd (**4**), 34th (**5**), and 71st (**6**).

The initial designs for light-infantry hats were described in 1772 as "black leather caps, with three chains round them [ostensibly to help guard against sword strokes], and a piece of plate upon the centre of the crown; in the front, G.R., a crown, and the number of the Regiment" (Simes 1781: 258). This seems to be the closest anyone came to a standardized, regulation description. In reality many regiments implemented their own designs or modified the originals, and consequently there was a great deal of variation among light-infantry caps by the outbreak of the American Revolutionary War.

Regardless of the initial regulations, it would appear that the light-infantry cap described in 1772 was not popular. In 1782 another Board of General Officers lambasted the headwear, stating that it was cumbersome and ineffective (Strachan 1975: 192). Needless to say, many light infantrymen had already come to a similar conclusion, with evidence that on campaign the original hard leather caps were replaced by cutdown felt hats or softer, collapsible leather caps.

1

2

3

4

5

6

Exterior of a reproduction cartridge pouch. The brass plate fixed to the pouch flap typically depicted either the royal cipher or the number or crest unique to that particular regiment, and tended to be smaller than the plates used by the regular companies. (Courtesy of the 4th Regiment of Foot)

high esteem by British light infantrymen during the American Revolutionary War and was frequently abandoned, so much so that it was formally removed from the uniform regulations in 1784. Exact descriptions of powder horns are scarce, but an American source describes one captured during the British retreat from Concord:

> [The horn] held just one pound of powder. It had a peculiar stopper (probably a spring snapper like some now known); and at the large end, on the underside (when hung over the shoulder), was engraved the English coat-of-arms, and on the upper side what they called the British ensign. The bottom of the horn was made of brass, saucer-

Interior of a reproduction cartridge pouch. This shows the wooden block that was drilled with holes to hold individual pre-made paper cartridges, each of which contained a musket ball and a measure of gunpowder. Beneath this block was storage space for tools that could be used for musket maintenance and to make fresh cartridges. (Courtesy of the 4th Regiment of Foot)

shaped, with a hole half an inch in diameter in the center serving as a tunnel to pour in the powder, with a wooden stopper. (Brown 1896: 297)

British soldiers had a variety of means for storing personal items, food, and the smaller tools of their trade. The largest was the knapsack. Early during the war these were typically square, with a single pouch, and made from leather such as goatskin, but as the conflict progressed knapsacks consisting of two pouches were adopted. These were typically made from linen and made waterproof with the oil of a reddish-brown paint. Ideally, one pouch was to be used to carry clothing "necessaries" such as spare shirts, stockings, and a forage cap, and the other for "dirty" items like spare shoes, soles, combs, and soap that would otherwise mark the clothing. They could also include personal items like dice, cards, books, and tobacco, though there are no lists of such objects, so ascertaining exactly what each soldier carried as personal belongings is guesswork at best. The knapsack possessed two shoulder straps and a third that could be buckled across the chest.

Interior of a reproduction cartridge box. Smaller than the pouch, the box provided extra cartridges, but was unpopular due to its propensity to flip over and dump its contents. On the occasions when it was worn it was usually slung over the shoulder. (Courtesy of the 4th Regiment of Foot)

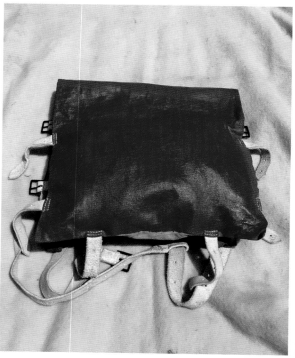
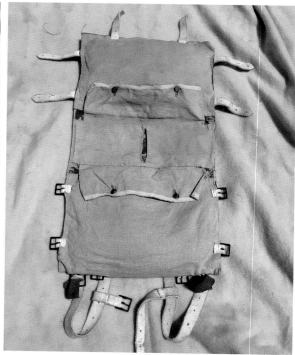

Reproduction knapsack, exterior and interior views. The reddish-brown hue comes from a waterproofing treatment. The two compartments allowed soldiers to keep personal items, spare clothing, and food separate. (Courtesy of the 4th Regiment of Foot)

As well as the knapsack, British soldiers were issued with the haversack. This was simply a linen bag with a nonadjustable strap. Smaller and lighter than the knapsack, the haversack was used for storing a few days' rations. Unlike the knapsack, the haversack would sometimes be carried into combat.

Besides haversacks and knapsacks, British infantry typically carried blanket rolls or slings on campaign. These often supplanted the knapsacks, with soldiers storing items inside the thick rolls of the blanket that was then

A view of the common contents of a light infantryman's haversack. Among the recreated items are his spare shoes, a forage cap for wearing when off duty, a shaving kit including brush and razor (even at the height of a hard campaign, a soldier was expected to remain clean-shaven), cup and spoon, spare undershirts, soap, and a pipe. (Courtesy of the 4th Regiment of Foot)

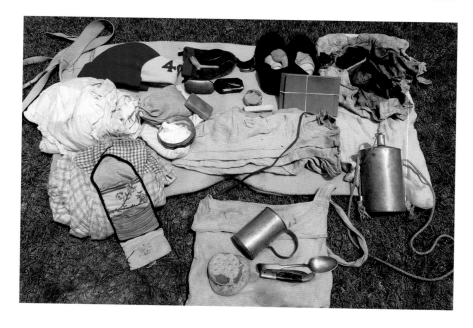

slung over one or both shoulders or attached to the knapsack by means of the strap that secured the roll.

British soldiers sometimes carried cups or their own drinking flasks as personal items for use in camp, but each man was issued with a water flask as part of his camp equipage. These were typically made of tin and varied in design, being secured over the shoulder with a length of narrow hemp cord. Wooden canteens were shipped to America in 1781, but too late for major campaigning. The light infantry and grenadiers of the 70th Foot, for example, are described in 1781 as having "a Wood Canteen; which sort are universally esteem'd by the Army here as far superior to the tin ones send from England … experience has convinced them they are far preferable to any other sort whatever" (WO 34/119: 85).

RECRUITMENT AND MOTIVATION

In a reversal of the concept of grenadiers being the tallest men in a battalion, the light infantry were ostensibly to be drawn from the shortest. There is some evidence that this practice was actually maintained in peacetime: the inspection of the 4th Regiment of Foot in 1774 revealed that the average height of men in the regiment's light-infantry company was 5ft 7in, 1in shorter than the average height of men in the "hatman" companies and 4in shorter than the average grenadier. Despite this, after fighting broke out the pressures of war made physical stature one of the last considerations for inclusion in the light companies. Speed and stamina, agility, marksmanship, and both discipline and an ability to think and act independently were the foremost prerequisites. British officers favored proven soldiers with combat experience for the flank companies, with Lieutenant-Colonel Thomas Musgrave, commanding officer of the 40th Foot, directing in 1777 that exemplary soldiers who had already served at least one year were to be considered for transfer to a light company (Spring 2008: 61). In 1768 Captain Bennett Cuthbertson opined that the light infantry should consist only of "chosen men, whose activity and particular talents for that duty should be the only recommendation to their appointment" (Cuthbertson 1776: 190). Officers seeking combat roles or the opportunity of advancement through action likewise sought out the lights; in 1777 Captain Colin Lindsay wrote of how he "desired to go into the light infantry, which is at present the most active service" in spite of the fact that he held the ostensibly more prestigious appointment of aide-de-camp (Lindsay 1861: 107). George Townshend, in a letter dated June 17, 1775, summed up the recruitment of light infantrymen perhaps most succinctly: "it is not a Short Coat or Half-Gaiters that makes a Light infantry man, but as you know, Sir, a confidence in his aim, and that stratagem in a personal conflict, which is derived from experience" (Amherst MSS).

Perhaps unsurprisingly, some commanders disapproved of the grouping of light companies together into battalions due to the fact that it deprived the "marching" regiments of their most active soldiers and skirmishers. Both the light and grenadier battalions would be replenished between campaigns with suitable soldiers from the regular infantry regiments, meaning that on campaign the regiments continued to experience a drain on their best men. This was a price that generals such as Howe appear to have been willing to pay.

The deployment of soldiers to Boston in the late 1760s proved to be an inauspicious renewal of relationships between American colonists and British regulars following the end of the Seven Years' War. Ostensibly there to maintain order in the fractious colony, British soldiers frequently became embroiled in brawls and bouts of intense antagonization with the locals, the most infamous of which led to the shootings in Boston on the night of March 5/6, 1770. Given the confrontational precedent set by British soldiers during their stay, it is perhaps unsurprising that the regulars and their colonial enemies rapidly developed a strong antipathy once active fighting broke out in New England in April 1775. British light infantry, however, frequently took their willingness to engage the enemy to new heights. During the surprise attack at Paoli on September 20, 1777, a British officer recalled how "the light infantry being ordered to form in front, rushed along the line putting to the bayonet all they came up with, and, overtaking the main herd of the fugitives, stabbed great numbers and pressed on their rear till it was thought prudent to order them to desist" (André 1903: 94). The light infantry appeared to take great pride in this bloody success, with some accounts claiming they added red hackles to their hats to commemorate the nighttime action. Though the exact provenance of such uniform modifications seems unclear, it is certain that an *esprit de corps* characterized by bloodthirsty elan was developing.

Following Paoli the Patriots dubbed the light infantry "bloodhounds," a nickname they seem to have embraced. It exemplified the mindset of the corps, and their enemies would at times recall the peal of hunting horns and the yelling and whooping of beaters preceding their attacks. Indeed, one light-infantry officer, Captain William Dansey, went so far as to claim in a

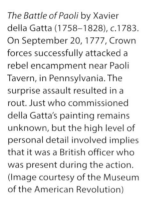

The Battle of Paoli by Xavier della Gatta (1758–1828), *c.*1783. On September 20, 1777, Crown forces successfully attacked a rebel encampment near Paoli Tavern, in Pennsylvania. The surprise assault resulted in a rout. Just who commissioned della Gatta's painting remains unknown, but the high level of personal detail involved implies that it was a British officer who was present during the action. (Image courtesy of the Museum of the American Revolution)

A detail from *The Battle of Paoli* by Xavier della Gatta, c.1783. Here we see British light infantrymen bayoneting fleeing or surrendering Continental Army soldiers. The light infantry constituted the first wave of the assault and launched their attack after having removed the flints from their muskets, forcing them to rely only on their bayonets. One British officer wrote of how the light infantry "rushed along the line putting to the bayonet all they came up with, and, overtaking the main herd of the fugitives, stabbed great numbers and pressed on their rear till it was thought prudent to order them to desist" (André 1903: 94). (Detail of *The Battle of Paoli*, Museum of the American Revolution)

letter to his mother, dated March 15, 1777, that fighting the Patriots was little different to hunting foxes back in England (Spring 2008: 253).

The *esprit de corps* enjoyed by the light infantry manifested itself in other ways. Desertion rates were lower than in other battalions throughout the war, and light infantrymen proved reluctant either to retreat or to surrender in the face of the enemy. At the battle of Germantown (October 4, 1777), the 2nd Battalion Light Infantry was on the receiving end of the Patriots' initial surprise attack. After re-forming following the flight of their piquets, the British light infantrymen returned the first volley and immediately charged the enemy at bayonet point. The Patriots rallied, counterattacked, and were in turn charged again by the light infantry, who had by then been hopelessly outflanked on either side. The 2nd Battalion was ordered to withdraw, but despite mounting casualties and the threat of complete encirclement, one British light-infantry officer, Lieutenant Martin Hunter of the 52nd Regiment of Foot's light company, recalled that "this was the first time we had ever retreated from the Americans, and it was with great difficulty that we could prevail on the men to obey our orders" (Hunter 1894: 34).

Captain Mathew Johnson of the 46th Regiment of Foot's light company reported a similar story during fighting at Harlem Heights on September 16, 1776, claiming that even the most badly wounded men in his company would not retreat when ordered to, but continued to fight (Spring 2008: 129). So great was the light infantry's zeal that, when rumors of a peace settlement began to circulate in 1778, they almost mutinied, burning effigies of the British Members of Parliament they believed to be responsible for seeking terms with the American rebels.

The light infantry's ferocity, at times spilling over into outright brutality, seems to have been shared and encouraged by their officers, at least at a company level. One light-infantry captain, William Glanville Evelyn of the 4th Foot, stated darkly that he hoped Britain's inhabitants would "permit us to restore to them the dominion of the country by laying it waste, and

Another detail from *The Battle of Paoli* by Xavier della Gatta, *c*.1783. Light infantry, including both British regulars and Loyalists of Major Patrick Ferguson's corps, are shown rushing on scattered pockets of rebels with fixed bayonets. The figure in the left foreground is likely Lieutenant Martin Hunter, who was wounded in the hand during the action. (Detail of The Battle of Paoli, Museum of the American Revolution)

almost extirpating the present rebellious race" (Evelyn 1879: 65). In a letter to his father, he wrote: "I hope before the end of it to be able to tell you that Boston, New York, Philadelphia, and all the capital towns on the Continent, are but stacks of chimneys" (Evelyn 1879: 71). Similarly, the accounts of Continental Army dragoons savaged during a surprise attack by the light infantry at Old Tappan on September 27, 1778 recalled how "none of the British officers entered the quarters of our Troops on this occasion, that no Stop might be put to the Rage and Barbarity of their Bloodhounds" (quoted in Stirling 1779: 293). Light-infantry officers were implicated by multiple survivors during the incident, one testifying that "he heard the British soldiers reply … that their captain had ordered them to stab all, and take no prisoners," while another claimed that "British soldiers, on entering the barn where they were, sent to know of their officer what they were to do with the two prisoners, who return for answer, that they were to kill every one of them" (quoted in Stirling 1779: 294).

Bloody ardor was also adopted by the light-infantry companies and ad hoc battalions in the American Provincial Corps. Emulating their brethren in the regulars, when a detachment of 20 Provincial light infantrymen were surrounded by Brigadier General Thomas Sumter's partisans while foraging in South Carolina on February 27, 1781, their commanding officer, Ensign Richard Cooper, replied to demands that he surrender by declaring that

D THE BATTLE OF PAOLI, SEPTEMBER 20, 1777

The British attack on Brigadier General Anthony Wayne's large Continental Army detachment near Paoli Tavern highlighted the combat abilities of British light infantry around the midpoint of the war – the British route march through the dark to surprise the rebels had been conducted with far greater efficiency than the march to Lexington and Concord two years earlier. Despite being forewarned about the British approach, Wayne was slow to take action, and the Continental

Army camp was still in a state of unpreparedness when the British attack, spearheaded by the light infantry, came sweeping out of the nearby forests.

According to one British officer, the lights massacred the rebel piquets at bayonet point and carried on into the camp, relying on close-quarter speed and aggression. The panic this caused led to the complete collapse of rebel resistance. Here we see light infantrymen dispatching the camp's piquets with bayonets and musket butts.

light infantry did not surrender (Braisted 2015). The little company proved themselves equal to the claim – forming a circle and using trees for cover, they held off Sumter's attack until more Loyalist light troops arrived to reinforce them.

The reputation of the light infantry also left a strong impression on their enemies. During one surprise attack, an unnamed rebel officer asked for the identity of his attackers. On being informed that they were British light infantry, he despairingly cried out "then we shall all be cut off" (quoted in Moore 1863: 96). Indeed, the mere appearance of light infantry could precipitate a complete rout. On December 29, 1778 the British recaptured Savannah after a slave guided a flanking force primarily consisting of light infantry through a swamp and into the rear of the Continental Army's lines. The sudden appearance of the British light infantrymen – and their immediate charge – led to an instant and total collapse of the rebel forces and the surrender of the town.

A reputation for ruthlessness inevitably resulted in reprisals, and at times a refusal by the light infantry to surrender was less due to the type of unit pride exhibited by the likes of Ensign Cooper, and more because of a belief that they would be shown no quarter. During the Patriot attack at Germantown on October 4, 1777, one Pennsylvanian officer told of how his men, knowing they were engaging a British light-infantry battalion, neither gave quarters nor expected any (McGuire 2000: 174). Similarly, Continental Army Brigadier General Anthony Wayne cited the earlier attack against his men at Paoli as the cause for unrestrained violence against the light infantry at Germantown: "our people remembering the action of the night of the 20th … pushed on with their bayonets and took ample revenge for that night's work. The rage and fury of the soldiers was not to be restrained for some time at least not until great numbers of the enemy fell by our bayonets" (quoted in Reed 1847: 320). On the opposite side, one British officer actually remembered hearing the shouts of the attacking rebels: "have at the Bloodhounds! Revenge Wayne's affair!" (Moorsom 1860: 21).

The light infantry had known all too well prior to Germantown that their previous actions and elite status meant they were a marked unit. Lieutenant Martin Hunter commented that as soon as the first shots were fired on the morning of the battle, "the battalion was out and under arms in a minute; so much had they in recollection Wayne's affair" (Hunter 1894: 33). Despite some initial panic, it didn't take the light infantry long to steady themselves and engage the enemy, in spite of the fact that the British knew that the nearest body of reinforcements were a mile to their rear.

While certainly convinced of their own abilities, the light infantry were not the only troops considered to be an elite within the British Army. The more senior of the flank companies, the grenadiers, were likewise formed into composite battalions for much of the war and were generally viewed by British officers as the more socially prestigious of the two arms. Chosen for their size and courage in the same way that light infantrymen were, on paper, chosen for their short stature, stamina, and marksmanship, in reality when formed into battalions the opposed flank companies sometimes fulfilled the same roles – that of shock troops deployed to break enemy lines, sometimes together, as at the battle of Brandywine (September 11, 1777). Perhaps unsurprisingly, the grenadiers and the lights developed an interesting camaraderie over the course of the war. Captain George Harris

of the 5th Regiment of Foot's grenadier company described emotionally how, when light and grenadier companies met:

> You would have felt too much to be able to express your feelings, on seeing with what a warmth of friendship our children (as we call the light infantry) welcomed us: one and all crying, "Let them come!" "Lead us to them, we are sure of being supported!" It gave me a pleasure too fine to attempt expressing; and if you see a stain on the paper, pray place the drops to the right motive, for the tears flowed even at the thought, so that I could not stop them. (Quoted in Lushington 1840: 86)

Hunter wrote of how "the grenadiers used to call us their children, and when we got more plunder than we wanted we always supplied our fathers" (Hunter 1894: 27). It seems that the idea of a familial bond between the two corps was a general one.

Other light infantry fighting for Great Britain

Crown forces in North America made frequent use of light and irregular troops well beyond the companies of the British Army's line regiments. The German state of Hessen-Cassel provided a corps of 500 rifle-armed *Jäger*, groups of Loyalist militia offered their services at various stages throughout the war, and bands of Loyalist rangers acted in concert with allied Native American war parties and, at times, companies of British regulars adapted to warfare on the frontier. Indeed, so great was the use of irregular fighting methods by the Crown and British allies across North America that it could be argued a greater emphasis was put on such means of fighting by British forces than it was by their opponents. Addressing the full gamut of Crown troops using light-infantry tactics is beyond the scope of this study, but it would be remiss not to include the provisional light battalions and the light troops of the American Provincial Corps, based as they were on those of the regular Army.

While Howe called for the creation of three light-infantry battalions from his regular light companies in 1776 (a fourth was listed, but never formed), other battalions and composite groupings of both British Army and Loyalist Provincial light infantry were established at various times during the American Revolutionary War. These provisional battalions were created on an ad hoc basis, in much the same way as the battalions of light infantry that had been formed for the Louisbourg and Quebec campaigns of 1758 and 1759.

E **OTHER LIGHT INFANTRY FIGHTING FOR THE BRITISH CROWN**

(1) Hessian *Jäger*, 1777

The *Jäger* corps, as it became known, originally composed of two companies of rifle-armed "hunters" belonging to the state of Hessen-Cassel, mustered into the British service with other Hessian troops in March 1776. In June that year they departed for North America, and were supplemented in 1777 with three more infantry companies and one mounted company, bringing their total to some 500 effectives. Modeled after the Prussian *Jäger* of the Seven Years' War, the Hessen-Cassel *Jäger* corps proved to be invaluable as light troops and skirmishers, frequently working alongside British light infantry and American Loyalist Provincials. Originally clad in green coats with red facings based on the Prussian style, these uniforms were largely worn out by early 1777 and were replaced that year with modified green Provincial coats supplied by Lieutenant-General Charles, Lord Cornwallis. The rifles used by the *Jäger*, made at Schmalkalden in Germany, had a 29in barrel and were .65 caliber.

While Hessians were the most numerous, other German states also included *Jäger* companies in the regiments supplied to assist British forces in North America. For example, one Brunswick regiment, Von Barner's Light Infantry, included its own *Jäger* company. The regiment was heavily involved during the Saratoga campaign of June–October 1777.

(2) Ranger, Butler's Rangers, 1777

Raised in 1777 by Loyalist Lieutenant-Colonel John Butler, Butler's Rangers was a Provincial regiment that saw action across the northern and northwestern frontier. Modeled after the famed ranger regiments of the Seven Years' War, the unit's operations revolved around raiding and irregular combat. On July 3, 1778 a force of rangers lured Continental Army troops into an ambush sprung by Native American allies at Wyoming, resulting in a complete rout. Allied with a number of different Native American tribes and Loyalist volunteers, ranger parties struck at pro-Congress frontier settlements such as Cherry Valley on November 11, 1778. The guerrilla tactics of the rangers forced Congress to relocate thousands of soldiers from the Eastern theaters to help protect the frontier communities over the course of the war.

The uniform worn by the men of Butler's Rangers remains a point of some debate, but the most likely evidence points to a green coat with white facings, a white woolen waistcoat, linen gaiter-trousers, and a round hat. Though irregular Loyalist volunteers sometimes adopted the warpaint and clothing of their Native American allies, there is no primary evidence to suggest that the rangers did likewise.

(3) Private, British Legion Light Infantry, 1780

The British Legion was a Loyalist Provincial regiment. The term "legion" was used to identify a combined-arms regiment consisting of cavalry, infantry, and sometimes light artillery. In effect it formed a small, self-contained strike force that proved invaluable to both sides during the mobile guerrilla warfare waged in the Carolinas and Virginia in 1780 and 1781. The British Legion, commanded by Lieutenant-Colonel Banastre Tarleton, was the most successful of these units.

The British Legion's light infantry were led for most of the war by Major Charles Cochran, a Scottish officer who had formerly served in the 4th Regiment of Foot. To maximize the British Legion's speed, Cochran regularly either had the light infantry double up with the dragoons on forced marches, or procured them their own horses, writing that "zealous for the honour of the Corps and to promote the service, the infantry have often rode over eighty miles in twenty-four hours without either bridle or saddle, and only a blanket and a piece of rope substituted … to surprise and beat the enemy" (quoted in Chamberlain 1891: 6).

British Legion light infantry wore green Provincial jackets with black facings (Carman 1984: 130). While some writers have them wearing the crested helmets famously adopted by the British Legion's dragoons, it seems more likely that they wore a light infantryman's leather cap with a brass "L" plate affixed to the front, possibly replaced on occasion by a simple round felt hat.

Partly cocked hat. These replaced the light-infantry caps at various points throughout the American Revolutionary War. At times the style was adopted by the whole army on campaign, as with Howe's forces in 1777. This cap is decorated with a feather and bearskin tuft, relatively common additions. The use of a green or red feather (rather than the more common black) is thought to have begun to appear from 1778 onwards. A later source describes how after the engagement at Old Tappan on September 27, 1778, Colonel John Maitland declared he would order the sporting of red feathers, with the 2nd Battalion adopting them while the 1st Battalion adopted green ones (Robertson 1948: 31). Lieutenant Martin Laye of the Royal Artillery described in 1778 how "the Light Infantry wear a green feather in their Caps & we the Grenadiers a White one in our Hatts" (Laye NAM 6807-154). (Courtesy of the 4th Regiment of Foot)

One such battalion was formed in the South from the light companies of the 16th and 71st Foot (both 1st and 2nd battalions) and the Provincials of the Prince of Wales's Volunteers. This small "battalion of light infantry had signalized themselves on many occasions" before their defeat at the battle of Cowpens on January 17, 1781 (Mackenzie 1787: 112). Similarly, in 1780 a battalion was formed purely from Loyalist light companies at New York, drawn from the King's American Regiment, the Loyal American Regiment, the 3rd Battalion of DeLancey's Brigade, and the 1st and 2nd battalions of the New Jersey Volunteers. This force was placed under the command of a light-infantry officer from the Brigade of Guards, Lieutenant-Colonel John Watson Tadswell Watson. Designated Provincial Light Infantry, they were deployed to support British forces in the South. The Provincials were heavily engaged at the battle of Eutaw Springs on September 8, 1781, losing almost half of their already depleted battalion.

Besides the provisional battalions, a number of the Loyalist Provincial regiments organized themselves along the lines of a complete light corps. This was most effectively implemented by the Queen's Rangers and the British Legion, both of which consisted of a mixture of light infantry and light cavalry (and, occasionally, small artillery pieces). The concept of a "legion" during the war was of a compact all-arms formation capable of conducting itself independently from the support of the main army, even in hostile territory. Intended to be highly mobile, the infantry arms of both the Queen's Rangers and the British Legion consisted entirely of light troops modeled after the light companies of regular Army regiments. Indeed, the first colonel of the Queen's Rangers was Robert Rogers, of Seven Years' War fame. For most of the war both the Queen's Rangers and the British Legion were commanded by two young, active, and aggressive British officers – Lieutenant-Colonel John Graves Simcoe and Lieutenant-Colonel Banastre Tarleton – both of whom proved to be among the most effective commanders of light troops during the war.

As well as the Provincial troops, regulars would sometimes be brigaded together outside of the regular light battalions. While mounting his expedition on June 7, 1781 to relieve the besieged Loyalist post at Ninety Six, Colonel Francis, Lord Rawdon formed his flank companies into an elite corps. Similarly, Lieutenant-General Charles, Lord Cornwallis occasionally formed a small battalion from available light companies during his Southern campaigns – four companies fought on the right of the British front line at Camden on August 16, 1780, where they helped rout the militia opposing them. In 1781, Rawdon formed a flank battalion by combining the light and grenadier companies of the 3rd, 19th, and 30th regiments of Foot. Commanded by Major John Majoribanks, this provisional battalion of regulars participated in the relief of Ninety Six (June 18, 1781) and the battle of Eutaw Springs (September 8, 1781), where they stood firm after much of the rest of the army had broken, withstanding a rebel cavalry charge and capturing prominent Continental Army officer Colonel William Washington before successfully mounting a counterattack that drove the rebels from the field.

OPERATIONS

The duties undertaken by the light infantry were perhaps the broadest of any experienced by British soldiers during the American Revolutionary War. They would act as foragers and provide protection to others bringing in supplies, constitute the vanguard, rearguard, and flankers when the army was on the move, and screen forces and provide outposts when encamped. When engaged in battle they could be called upon to act as skirmishers, line-of-battle infantry, or shock troops who spearheaded assaults. They led raids and surprise attacks, conducted ambushes, and could harry defeated foes for miles, or rush to the assistance of embattled allies. There was almost no tactical situation throughout the American Revolutionary War that a light company or battalion did not experience. Consequently, they were relied upon by British commanders across the globe during the wider conflict, from North America to Gibraltar to India.

"Famous providers"

Keeping Crown forces fed throughout their campaigns in North America was no mean feat. While the British Army relied on a system of local contractors, merchants, and shipping produce from Britain, food and other supplies were also acquired through a combination of foraging and looting. The light infantry proved to be adept at both. Light companies would frequently be picked both for the task of foraging, and to protect other parties of foragers while out beyond the lines. Directives recorded in an orderly book dated September 4, 1777, for example, describe how "each Corps will send an Officer and a sufficient Number of Men with Haversacks to-morrow morning at 7, to Lord Cornwallis's Quarters, to receive one day's Flour. A Commissary will be there to conduct them, and two Companies from 2d. Light Infantry are to attend as a Covering party" (quoted in Kembel 1884: 486). Fifteen days later, an officer's diary entry notes how three companies of light infantry had "taken possession of 4000 barrels of flour at Valley Forge" along with "a great quantity of camp kettles, axes, horseshoes, nails &c." (André 1903: 92). Such activities constituted the day-to-day operations that helped to keep 18th-century armies supplied in the field.

Accounts also make clear just how rampant a problem theft and looting posed throughout the war. In keeping with other armies since time immemorial, British soldiers were prone to taking what didn't belong to them, while either on the march or ensconced in camp. This could range from stealing vegetables from a garden to ransacking and torching homesteads. The light battalions were especially noted for their rapacity, given that alongside the light dragoons they often constituted the vanguard of the advanced corps (usually the largest British column operating closest to the enemy) on the line of march, and therefore got the first, richest pickings. Major Patrick Ferguson bitterly noted the excess of fresh food the light infantry could at times enjoy while the rest of the army went without (Urwin 2019: 11).

Records of orders issued from headquarters revealed the efforts of British commanders to curtail their men's unlawful activities, the former being especially mindful of the need to not make further enemies out of American colonists by laying waste to their homes and livestock. One set of brigade orders issued to the light infantry spoke of a particularly high number of complaints being directed toward the light infantry by local inhabitants, and warned officers to be on their guard against looting (Coote 2011). Light-infantry officer Lieutenant-Colonel Robert Abercromby issued a set of orders while the lights were encamped near New York on November 29, 1778, which stated that he would closely prosecute thieves and urged company commanders to give up their men (Coote 2011).

Such directives came from the top of the British Army's command structure in North America, with the commander-in-chief, Lieutenant-General Sir Henry Clinton, issuing similar orders almost as soon as he arrived in the South during the British attempt to retake Charleston in March–May 1780. In their efforts to curtail looting, officers would post soldiers to houses along the route of march with the intention of protecting them

Sketch by Lieutenant Richard St. George Mansergh showing him mocking captured prisoners. Both officers and enlisted men in British light-infantry companies frequently showed antipathy toward their opponents. (Harlan Crow Library, Dallas, Texas)

from passing opportunists, with one order even giving them the right to kill any marauders. Clearly such guards were of limited use – on November 16, 1779, two light infantrymen of the 57th Regiment of Foot, Charles Dortarly and Peter Deves, went on trial for having robbed a house while ostensibly being posted to guard it (Coote 2011).

Orders also frequently demanded that light-infantry officers remain among the tents or huts being utilized by their men, rather than seek more comfortable accommodation nearby, as was common practice. While this was partly to allow them to take immediate command in case of sudden action, it was also intended to give them better oversight of their men's activities. Again, however, such precautions against indiscipline failed to take full effect, at least in part because the captains and lieutenants in direct command of the light companies often seem to have turned a blind eye to what were often termed their men's "irregularities." Indeed, Lieutenant Hunter appears to have taken active pride in the looting abilities of his own light infantrymen, writing that

> the 52nd Light Infantry were famous providers. They were good hands at a grab. Grab was a favorite expression among the light infantry, and meant any plunder taken by force; a lob, when you got it without an opposition. And I am very certain there never was a more expert set than the light infantry at either grab, lob, or gutting a house. (Hunter 1894: 27)

Ultimately, the threats of senior British officers regarding looting were rarely carried out. Soldiers, especially elite ones such as the light infantry, were at a premium in North America, and most British commanders weren't willing to hang such men or administer debilitating floggings because of excessive larceny. At a company level, junior officers appear to have preferred to protect their men and deal with incidents "in-house" rather than put them through the British Army's formal courts martial. Occasional examples were made – on September 15, 1777 a light infantryman and a grenadier were hanged, in the words of Major John André, "for plunder" (André 1903: 89) – but such punishments were comparatively rare.

Screening

Besides foraging, one of the most common tasks undertaken by British light infantry in North America was screening the army, both in camp and on the march. This duty, like many others, they shared with the cavalry. Indeed, it wasn't uncommon for the distinction between light cavalry and light infantry to become blurred while on campaign. The light-infantry battalions would occasionally provide companies of mounted infantrymen to supplement the Crown's mounted forces, and sometimes operated out-and-out as dragoons, as some members from the 71st Foot's light company likely did during the siege of Savannah (September 16–October 18, 1779), even going so far as to acquire a shipment of uniforms from the 17th Light Dragoons. Similarly, light infantry would at times "double up" with dragoons on their mounts if speed was essential, as the British Legion's light infantry often did with their own unit's dragoons while fighting in the South. It is interesting to note the similarities between some styles of light-infantry cap, such as the ones sported by the 5th Foot, and the helmets worn by light dragoons.

Protecting other British forces during the American Revolutionary War was both a vigorous and arduous task. It was not uncommon for encampments regularly to be threatened or marching columns attacked, whether by militia or the Continental Army. Often acting as the vanguard and flankers, light infantry would be sent to intercept any such threat. On June 22, 1777, Major André recorded how a force of rebels "fell in with the column of march" and "attacked the Light Infantry but were immediately driven back; they however, shifted their position from one thicket to another and hung upon the flanks and rear for some distance. They killed or wounded about twenty of our people and a woman, a Grenadier's wife" (André 1903: 43). On September 3, André again recalls the light infantry protecting the column and clearing a path, writing how they

> fell in with a body of about 500 rebels … they disposed of themselves amongst some trees by the roadside, and gave a heavy fire as our troops advanced, but upon being pressed ran away and were pursued above two miles … of the chasseurs [*Jäger*] and light infantry, the only troops engaged, three or four were killed and twelve or fourteen wounded. (André 1903: 80–81)

It is worth noting the impressive stamina frequently displayed by light infantrymen throughout the war. On December 6, 1777, André's diary records two separate instances of the light infantry being involved in running battles. In the first case, the light infantry of the Brigade of Guards combined with the light troops of the Queen's Rangers to attack rebels firing from "a woody ridge … the light infantry of the guards with great activity and ardor ran round the foot of the ridge and came upon their flank in time enough to intercept a few in their flight" (André 1903: 124). This exploit was followed by a rebel counterattack in which "the light infantry of the guards were very briskly attacked about an hour after taking post, by very superior numbers, but they maintained their ground and repulsed the enemy" (André 1903: 125). At the same time the 2nd Battalion Light Infantry "had also a skirmish with Morgan's Battalion of riflemen. Only five companies were brought to action, and of these from circumstances of ground, &c., which we are unacquainted with, three only could act with vigor; these drove them a considerable distance and threw them into confusion" (André 1903: 126).

Fighting after prolonged or intensive marches was par for the course for most light infantrymen. At the battle of Long Island on August 27, 1776 – the first test of Howe's army following the evacuation of Boston and the time spent drilling at Halifax – the light-infantry battalions provided the vanguard on a 19-mile night march through difficult terrain, successfully leading the main part of the British forces in a wide maneuver that went undetected by the Continental Army elements posted on the Guam and Brooklyn Heights. During the ensuing battle the light infantry remained at the front of the British attack, driving confused and scattering revolutionary forces before them and suffering among the highest casualties of any British brigade during the battle. Similarly, Lieutenant Hunter claimed that during a forced march in May 1778, the 52nd Foot's light infantry covered 60 miles in 24 hours without a single soldier dropping out from fatigue. By way of explanation he stated that his men "were in good wind, as we generally marched out of Philadelphia every day ten or twelve miles to cover the market people coming in" (Hunter 1894: 40–41).

Speed and stamina proved vital not just during an attack, but also when it came to withdrawal. During the British efforts to retake the Caribbean

A VIEW IN AMERICA IN 1778

island of St. Lucia from the French in December 1778, an unexpected French advance through forested terrain caught the light infantry by surprise. Luckily, "an exertion of their usual agility" allowed most of them to escape to the nearby British defensive lines, where the French attack was repulsed (Whinyates 1898: 97).

Guarding British encampments was also a hazardous and, at times, draining duty for the light companies. André's only diary entry for October 24, 1777, reads "several shots were exchanged in the morning between the rebel patrols and those of the jagers and light infantry" (André 1903: 122). On December 24, 1777, he wrote that "in the morning a few shots were fired by sentries of the 1st light infantry, at a party of the rebels who passed along their front" (André 1903: 132). One light officer, Lieutenant Richard St. George Mansergh, writing a letter to his beloved on the night of October 2, 1777, described how "there has been firing this Night all around the Centrys – which seems as if they [the Patriots] endeavour to feel our situation … I am fatigued & must sleep" (quoted in Abbatt 1905: 146).

Skirmishing

When battle was actively joined, light infantry tended to be employed by their commanders in any of three particular roles. The first involved perhaps the best-known method of combat for light troops – skirmishing. When this was the case, the company or battalion in question would shake itself out into an "extended file" of skirmishing pairs, more irregular than

An original light-infantry cap believed to have belonged to an officer of the 9th Regiment of Foot. While the providence of this is uncertain, it does give an indication of the variety of styles adopted (Image courtesy of the National Army Museum, London)

the open-order tactics usually employed by a line battalion. These duos of light infantrymen would take advantage of whatever cover was nearby – trees, undergrowth, fences, walls – or, if nothing was available, kneel or drop to the ground. Having done so they would conduct an irregular fire, pressing forward where possible. If their opponents were close-order infantry, this method of fighting could be sufficient to win the engagement. If the light infantry were fighting fellow-skirmishers, usually in woodland terrain, the British would frequently resort to a bayonet charge to decide the encounter, almost invariably leading to the opposition's flight (though whether they came back again after the charge was spent was another matter).

Such forest engagements, typically known as "bushfighting," consistently proved to be among the sternest tests British light infantry faced during the American Revolutionary War. British officers commented on the superior abilities displayed by their opponents during woodland combat, and it was

F

BRITISH LIGHT INFANTRY AT BIRMINGHAM HILL, SEPTEMBER 11, 1777

Soon after the beginning of the battle of Brandywine, the 1st and 2nd battalions Light Infantry assaulted the 3rd Virginian Regiment of the Continental Army at a Quaker church known as the Birmingham Meetinghouse. After driving the Continentals back, the lights proceeded to attack uphill against a Continental Army division, eventually likewise forcing them back and overrunning a battery of artillery. Throughout the battle, much of which was conducted in forested or swampy terrain, the light battalions and supporting companies of *Jäger* acted in a decentralized fashion, individual companies operating at the behest of their captains and lieutenants in order to overcome obstacles and outflank the enemy.

Here we see three companies of the 1st Battalion Light Infantry (from the 17th, 33rd, and 38th regiments of Foot) attacking the Virginians of Brigadier General Charles Scott's

4th Virginia Brigade. The 17th Foot had initially come upon the Continentals but waited until the arrival of the 33rd and 38th Foot before beginning their attack, with half of the light company providing fire support for the 1st Grenadier Battalion attacking farther to their right. One lights officer, Captain William Scott, described his men going down on their knees and stomachs to return fire, and in this way forcing back multiple attacks (Spring 2008: 186). Seeing the commander of the leftmost company of the grenadier battalion to their right close by, the light-infantry officers persuaded him to bring his company (the 43rd Foot's) to their aid. At this point, assailed across the line farther to the left by the rest of the 1st Battalion Light Infantry and the 2nd Battalion Light Infantry, the Continentals began to give way. The light companies charged and overran five cannon which had been abandoned after their limber horses were killed (Spring 2008: 186–87). The silencing of these guns allowed a general advance and the rout of the Continental Army defenders.

very much intended that the British light infantry should match the enemy in their own style of warfare.

Whether or not they were used as skirmishers, it should not be imagined that the light-infantry battalions necessarily always operated as a fixed force when battle was joined. During the battle of Brandywine, for example, as the lights engaged Continental Army infantry forces on a hill beyond Birmingham Meetinghouse their companies operated largely independently of one another, sometimes separated by terrain and each acting entirely on the initiative of its own officers. Such a detached form of command enabled the light companies to offer better support to the rest of the army than the standard representation of a static battalion formation might imply.

Properly utilized cover was deemed of key importance during skirmishing. Officers added new vocabulary relating to the use of trees during woodland battles (Spring 2008: 254). Indeed the phrase "to tree" is one that appears in Howe's 1774 *Discipline*, showing that the exercises conducted at Salisbury and in Richmond Park were not merely a case of open-order maneuvers, but a step along the path towards a broadly understood series of light-infantry doctrines which, even if they weren't committed to a formal military treatise by Howe, were effectively put into practice by the British Army in North America.

Formed combat

While the light infantry were usually envisioned as being a force tailored to the conduct of skirmishing and irregular warfare, British generals such as William Howe conceived of them as an all-round elite capable of performing almost any military task required of them. Consequently, the light battalions were employed as regular British infantry during the American Revolutionary War as frequently as they were used as skirmishers, if not more so.

Such a role is not as much of a contrast as it may first appear. The standard tactics of British regulars in North America, even for the line companies, were based upon an open-order formation two ranks deep that was encouraged to make use of cover when necessary. Consequently, it should come as no surprise that the light infantry were capable of acting as a line-of-battle force with as much effectiveness as when they were employed as skirmishers. Both the 1st and 2nd battalions Light Infantry found themselves resisting Washington's attack at Germantown in open-order lines and launching multiple bayonet charges in an effort to keep the Continental Army forces at bay. Indeed, the bayonet charge and their general use as shock troops made the light battalions at times seem more akin to "heavy infantry" like their fellow flank corps, the grenadiers. Howe seems always to have envisioned his light troops mounting frontal attacks on defended positions: the review held in Richmond Park following the training at Salisbury included a mock attack by light infantry on a defended hilltop, even simulating the shock inflicted by the enemy's volley by having the attackers "checked" during the charge.

Frequently, engagements during the American Revolutionary War required the light battalions to fight both as skirmishers and as a formed force. The battle of Harlem Heights offers one such example. On the morning of September 16, 1776, piquets of the 2nd Battalion Light Infantry spotted and engaged a small advanced force of rebel rangers led by Lieutenant Colonel Thomas Knowlton probing the British lines. Several companies of British light infantry responded to the threat and attacked the enemy. They conducted a brisk skirmish for around a half-hour across woodland, fields, and farmsteads – just the sort of terrain Howe had envisioned during his demonstration in Richmond Park.

Not for the first time, the light infantry's impetuosity got the better of them. According to Rawdon they pursued the enemy too far. Finding themselves almost surrounded by a lure set by Washington, the lights counterattacked so ferociously, according to Rawdon, that they initially drove the rebels right back to their lines (Nelson 2005: 48). Washington responded by feeding more soldiers into the engagement, and the lights, though now reinforced by the 3rd Battalion Light Infantry and the 42nd Foot, were forced to make a stand in a buckwheat field against almost double their number. After over an hour of fighting and with ammunition running low they conducted an orderly withdrawal, with the revolutionaries taking the opportunity to likewise break off the engagement.

Early on in the day's fighting Washington's Adjutant General, Colonel Joseph Reed, remembered how the lights "in the most insulting manner sounded their bugle horns as is usual after a fox chase. I never felt such

Sketch depicting a light-infantry officer, Lieutenant Richard St. George Mansergh, refusing a cloak in a storm, by Mansergh himself. A pair of greatcoats was issued to each company in a regular British battalion, and rotated between piquets in inclement weather. (Harlan Crow Library, Dallas, Texas)

a sensation before – it seemed to crown our disgrace" (quoted in Reed 1847: 237). While in reality it was more likely that the bugles were being sounded simply to rally the scattered British infantry, such an act was in keeping with the aggressive spirit of the "bloodhounds."

There was a worry among British officers that the policy of open-order fighting and loose bayonet assaults practiced in North America would ultimately prove detrimental were the British Army to encounter opponents using European close-order tactics. A number of commentators attributed the British defeat at the battle of Cowpens to the open order used by the British line battalions, claiming they were unable to withstand the "shock" of a sudden bayonet or cavalry charge. While such assaults by rebel forces had been almost unheard of at the start of the war, they began to occur with greater regularity as the Continental Army gained experience and confidence. Some officers worried about what would happen if British troops used to fighting in open and extended order came up against fully formed French infantry (Urban 2007: 305).

In reality, the rare engagements between French and British infantry during the American Revolutionary War didn't expose any particular mismatch between the two, especially where the light infantry were concerned. The lights won a clear victory over French troops on St. Lucia on December 18, 1778. On October 24, ten line regiments and their attendant flank companies were sent on Major-General James Grant's expedition to recapture the Caribbean island. While operating there a strong French relief force attacked a British detachment holding Vigie Peninsula, which included a number of the veteran light companies. The French attacked

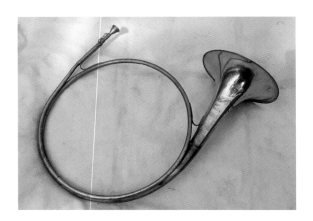

Replica light-infantry horn. There appear to have been a variety of wind instruments employed by light companies, from French horns and bugles to German hunting horns. Officers also used whistles to help issue commands to soldiers spread out through difficult terrain. (Courtesy of the 4th Regiment of Foot)

in assault columns – ideal targets for the Royal Artillery, particularly the enfilading batteries of heavy 18-pounders. While the French were under a barrage of shot, later sources describe how the light infantry used cover to harass the columns, occasionally threatening a bayonet charge if the enemy attempted to form line, and withdrawing if the enemy charged only to launch new ambushes later on (Clayton 2006: 63).

Sergeant-Major Thorne of the 5th Foot, present at the battle, told of how the regulars in his own regiment also supported the light companies with an irregular fighting style (Urban 2007: 306). Here we see the light troops putting into practice the method of fighting they had almost perfected in North America, using their speed, effective cover, and irregular fire to confound the enemy. Furthermore, it was a method of fighting the regular "hatman" companies were able and willing to emulate. The danger the lights posed went beyond that of just skirmishers – the threat of a bayonet charge proved their abilities as shock troops. Another source gives a similar narrative of the engagement at Vigie, claiming that by "advancing in skirmish order and keeping themselves always under cover, the light companies maintained at close range the most destructive fire on the Heavy French columns ... At last one of the enemy's battalions fairly gave way and the light companies

G | LIGHT INFANTRY NCOs AND MUSICIANS

(1) Musician, 40th Foot, 2nd Battalion Light Infantry, 1777

While initially listed on the rolls as "drummers," the musicians of the light companies during the American Revolutionary War employed a range of wind instruments for signaling commands. The musician here carries a large French-style horn which could be slung over the shoulder, thus ensuring it wasn't too much of an encumbrance in difficult terrain. He is depicted at the battle of Germantown, where a surprise attack by Washington's Continental Army was initially met by the light infantry. The heavy morning mist made command and control difficult, further underlining the importance of trumpet and bugle calls.

There was no standardized wind instrument used by all light companies, and the exact definitions of what today constitutes a trumpet, horn, or bugle wasn't familiar to 18th-century sources. German post-horns were popular among the light companies, especially the Hanoverian bugle-horn (*Halbmondblaser*). Pitched in the key of D and with a crook to reach down to C, it was used by British light-dragoon regiments in 1764 and eventually found its way into the light infantry. The *Halbmond* – meaning crescent – was typically made of copper and slung with a strap over the shoulder.

(2) Corporal, 52nd Foot, 2nd Battalion Light Infantry, 1777

This corporal of the 52nd Foot displays the uniform modifications introduced for the campaigns of 1777, namely his waistcoat worn as a jacket, with sleeves sewn on, and a felt hat that replaced his light-infantry cap, cocked up at one side. His rank is displayed by a single silk epaulet on his shoulder.

(3) Sergeant, Brigade of Guards Light Company, 1780

This Brigade of Guards NCO belongs to the 3rd Regiment of Foot Guards, later known as the Scots Guards. One of three regiments of Foot Guards during the American Revolutionary War, the Guards units required the sovereign's express permission to be deployed overseas. On February 13, 1776, the Foot Guards were ordered to detach 15 privates from each of the 64 companies of the three regiments. Assigned officers and formed into ten companies (including, for the first time, a light company), the composite force departed for New York on May 2, 1776. Aware of the conditions in North America, they modified their uniforms in line with the more lightweight style already adopted by British regiments fighting in the colonies. During the conflict several regular companies were converted into an additional light and grenadier company.

Major-General Edward Mathew commanded the Brigade of Guards and was responsible for outfitting its light companies, but relatively little evidence of their appearance remains. This light-infantry sergeant, identified by his 3rd Guards waist sash, is shown wading into the Catawba River in South Carolina during a forced crossing on February 1, 1781. Lieutenant-General Charles O'Hara described the river as extremely wide, quick, and deep, with numerous rocks and a steep, forested bank opposite (Rogers 1964: 175). Led by Lieutenant-Colonel Hall of the 3rd Guards, the light-infantry company spearheaded the attack on the opposite bank. They passed through the 500yd ford, which at its center was about 4ft deep. Men held onto one another's shoulders for support, while carrying their unloaded muskets and cartridge pouches on their shoulders. Eventually reaching the other bank, they were able to form up and advance with the bayonet, helping to drive off the defenders and allow the main British army to cross after them. Lieutenant-Colonel Hall was killed during the attack.

followed them to complete the rout with the bayonet" (Fortescue 1911: 269). Ultimately, three assaults on the British positions were defeated, costing the French force well over 1,000 killed or wounded.

Special operations

In keeping with Howe's view of his light infantry as the elite of the army, the light battalions would frequently lead what we might today term "special operations." It was common for sections of the main British army operating in North America to be detached to launch surprise attacks on isolated rebel forces or conduct raids against centers of rebel activity. Two of the most famous such operations occurred in September 1777 near Paoli Tavern and in September 1778 at Old Tappan. In both engagements the light infantry led a surprise attack and inflicted heavy casualties on an unsuspecting rebel force. Both engagements led to claims of atrocity being leveled by Congress.

The attributes that made the men of the light-infantry battalions effective troops lent themselves to such operations. Accustomed to hard, fast marches and maneuvering at night, they made for an effective vanguard and their confidence with the bayonet, not to mention their fearsome reputation, made them ideal shock troops. Contrasting the effectiveness of the British attacks at Paoli and Old Tappan with the difficulties experienced at the start of the war during the raid on Lexington and Concord shows how much the king's soldiers, and the light troops especially, developed over the first few years of the American Revolutionary War.

Light infantry were also in the vanguard of the British expedition commanded by Major-General Charles Grey that burned the privateer base at New Bedford on September 6, 1778, and Provincial light troops constituted most of Major Patrick Ferguson's corps during his successful raid on Little Egg Harbor, New Jersey, on October 15, 1778. In 1781 both the 1st and 2nd battalions Light Infantry were attached to Major-General William Phillips' expedition into Virginia, where they spearheaded raids and participated in the battle of Blandford on April 25. They were part of the British army that was besieged at Yorktown, and were to spearhead the final breakout effort across the York River on October 16, 1781, before bad weather aborted the operation.

Throughout the war British commanders in all theaters turned to the light infantry as soldiers of choice when it came to high-risk operations. Their involvement in actions such as the ones at Paoli and Old Tappan further cemented the view of them as elite troops, and pushed rebel antipathy toward them to new heights.

H **THE ATTACK AT OLD TAPPAN, SEPTEMBER 27, 1778**
Almost a year to the day after the successful British attack on unsuspecting rebel forces at Paoli, the light infantry repeated the trick near Old Tappan, in New Jersey. A force of over 100 Continental Army dragoons was caught sleeping in billets close to a bridge over the Hackensack River. The British achieved total surprise, putting many of the dragoons to the bayonet before they even realized they were under attack.

The operation, commanded by Major-General Charles Grey of Paoli fame, was spearheaded by six companies of light infantry led by Lieutenant-Colonel John Maitland and another six led by Major Turner van Straubenzee. Guided by over a dozen local Loyalists, they encircled the barns and houses where the dragoons were billeted and silenced several groups of pickets. Grey himself led a small group of light infantrymen toward the house of Cornelius Haring, where the detachment's officers were spending the night. They silenced the guards, while Straubenzee's light infantry killed or captured the officers within. With the enemy's commanders dealt with, the lights proceeded to move from barn to barn where the six dragoon troops were billeted, bayoneting many despite their attempts to surrender. The operation was a complete success, but provided a propaganda coup for Congress, who decried it as a massacre.

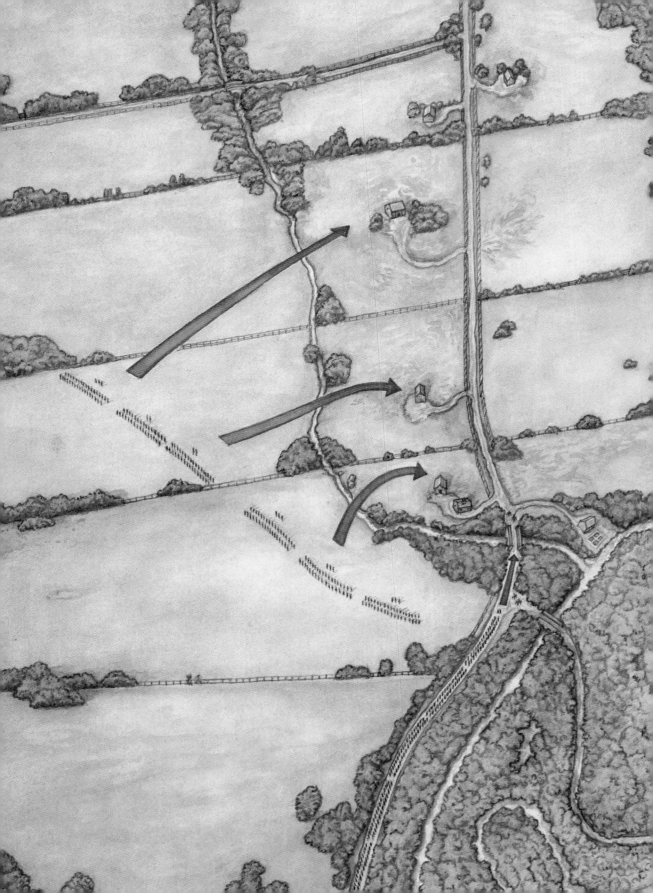

IMPACT AND INFLUENCE

Light-infantry influence on the wider British Army

After evacuating Boston in April 1776 the British forces, now commanded by General William Howe, sailed for Halifax. Once there Howe set out to remake them thoroughly in the image of what he believed would be a more effective "American army." Light-infantry doctrines and his past experiences fighting with the lights in North America clearly permeated many of his changes. The regular "hatman" companies of the line regiments were instructed in open-order drills and how to maneuver at pace. Uniforms were modeled after the style of the light infantry, with shorter coats, cutdown hats, and less lace. Officers shed many symbols of their rank, such as the metallic gold and silver lace and gorgets, learning from the heavy casualties inflicted on their corps during the battle of Bunker Hill (June 17, 1775). The efforts seem to have been effective – the casualties inflicted on British officers at Bunker Hill ultimately accounted for one-eighth of all losses suffered during the entire eight years of the war.

The light infantry continued to influence uniform modifications throughout the British army in North America. In preparation for his campaign into the northern wilderness in 1777, a British officer, Lieutenant Thomas Anbury, recorded that Major-General John Burgoyne directed the regiments under his command to "reduce the men's coats into jackets, and their hats into caps as it will be more convenient for wood service, that when the army take the field, they will in a manner be all light infantry" (Anbury 1789: 197–98). Likewise, during the Philadelphia campaign of 1777–78, Howe oversaw a flurry of uniform changes that modeled regular companies after the light infantry more closely than ever before, modifying cocked hats and wearing waistcoats rather than the regimental jackets.

It should be noted that variation abounded across the British military during the American Revolutionary War era, and exceptions to uniform rules and regulations existed in almost every imaginable sense. When factoring in the frequent copying of light-infantry uniform styles by the rest of the army on campaign it can further add to the confusion. There may be little way, for example, to tell a grenadier of the 20th Foot during the Saratoga campaign of June–October 1777 from a light infantryman at a glance, the grenadier wearing as he did a shortened jacket, tomahawk, gaiter-trousers, the felt cap worn by most soldiers under Burgoyne's command, and the shoulder wings that grenadiers shared with the light infantry. In this case belt color, the possibility of a grenadier's fuze box, or the long hair queue bound up beneath the cap (a style often affected by the grenadier companies, but sometimes also light infantry) would likely be the only distinctions.

The Continental Army's response

Given the active role played by British light infantry, it should come as little surprise that the Continental Army sought to implement its own light companies in its regular battalions. From 1777 onwards these units were seasonally raised and brigaded together into the Continental Army's light-infantry corps. While such a lack of continuity seems to have initially

Sketch by British light-infantry officer Richard St. George Mansergh, entitled *Virginian Rifleman*. Rifle-armed militia and the companies of riflemen raised by Congress were the nemesis of the British light infantry throughout the war. Here we see one such American clad in the popular irregular dress of a hunting shirt and broad-sided hat. Interestingly, in the wake of the battle of Long Island one Continental Army officer, Lieutenant Jasper Ewing, described how "several companies of their Light Infantry are cloathed exactly as we are, in hunting shirts and trowsers" (quoted in Johnston 1878: 50). Aping colonial dress was certainly uncommon among British light infantry. (Harlan Crow Library, Dallas, Texas)

curtailed their effectiveness as a cohesive fighting force, by the midpoint of the war they had begun to establish themselves as a true answer to their Crown forces counterparts.

In 1779 Brigadier General Anthony Wayne, a man who had been on the receiving end of the British light infantry on a number of occasions, was given command of the Continental Army's light-infantry corps. He proceeded to employ them just as British commanders had, in a daring, aggressive surprise assault on the unsuspecting British garrison of Stony Point, New York, on July 16, 1779. The Continental Army light infantry's success, gained with the bayonet, did much to establish their reputation. By the time of the siege of Yorktown the Continentals were described as having arrived "with the tread of veterans, colors flying, drums beating, and planted their standards on the parapet" (Johnston 1881: 135). They participated in the successful capture of one of the redoubts, again attacking with unloaded muskets and fixed bayonets, emphasizing the daring spirit and aggression that came to be the hallmark of light infantry on both sides throughout the war.

CONCLUSION

The end of the American Revolutionary War marked a break in the development of Britain's light infantry. While the light companies in the regular regiments were not disbanded as they had been at the end of the Seven Years' War, little was done to expand further on the important role light troops had played during the conflict. A lack of understanding regarding the best use of light infantry contributed to the difficulties in which the British Army found itself during the opening stages of the conflict with revolutionary France. As had been the case in the early 1770s, lessons would have to be relearned.

Fortunately, there were a number of excellent teachers. While officers such as Gage and Howe had come to appreciate light infantry during the Seven Years' War and had then brought their experience to bear during the American Revolutionary War, so veterans of the conflict in the New World helped to expand the British Army's light-infantry doctrine during the Napoleonic era. Most celebrated among their number was Lieutenant-General Sir John Moore, who had joined the British Army as a junior officer in 1776 and earned plaudits for his actions during the defeat of the rebels' Penobscot expedition in July–August 1779. In 1803, Moore took a post at Shorncliffe training camp in Kent and set about drilling a brigade in light-infantry concepts. The 52nd Foot, at that point commanded by Moore, was redesignated a light-infantry regiment, intended to function as both line and light troops, much as the composite battalions had during the American Revolutionary War. Other regiments followed and, along with the creation of the "Experimental Corps of Riflemen," the light infantry grew to comprise an entire division by the height of the Peninsular War (1807–14). While Moore's emphasis on promoting individual initiative, a more lenient system of discipline and closer ties between officers and enlisted ranks all helped to make the newer light regiments into an elite fighting force, there is no doubt that the concepts he developed had first been practiced effectively during the Seven Years' War and the American Revolutionary War.

Even before the first clashes in New England in 1775, British commanders were well aware that combat in North America required methods less commonly seen on most European battlefields. Far from being a hidebound institution that refused to adapt or accept its own shortcomings, the British Army during the American Revolutionary War embraced efforts that would better help it defeat the colonial rebellion. The concepts surrounding light infantry were diffused throughout Crown forces in North America, and consistently influenced everything from uniforms to Army-wide tactics.

While militarily successful, the problems faced by the British Army during the American Revolutionary War could not be solved through the tactical application of light infantry. In some ways the light battalions exemplified the British Army during the conflict in a more general sense; often successful on the battlefield but overly aggressive and thinly stretched, their efforts would ultimately fail to convince a critical number of Americans to submit to Crown authority. Regardless of Britain's wider failings during the Revolutionary War, however, there can be no doubt that the light infantry were one of the war's most battle-hardened, effective, and elite fighting forces. They were, in the words of a light-infantry sergeant, Thomas Sullivan, "the front going out, and the rear coming home" (Sullivan 1779: 151).

Miniature portrait of an unidentified British officer, believed to be a member of the light company of the 15th Regiment of Foot, c.1777. The hat cocked up on one side only may have been retained by these regiments in 1778 following their redeployment to the West Indies. (Courtesy of Donald D. Donohue/Americana Antiques LLC)

APPENDIX: Organizational timeline of the regular light-infantry battalions

May 14, 1776: Major-General William Howe authorizes the creation of two light-infantry battalions while at Halifax, Nova Scotia. The 1st Battalion, commanded by Major Thomas Musgrave of the 64th Foot and Major Thomas Dundas of the 65th Foot, is initially composed of nine companies of light infantry drawn from the 4th, 5th, 10th, 17th, 22nd, 23rd, 27th, 35th, and 38th regiments of Foot. The 2nd Battalion, commanded by Major John Maitland of the Marines and Major Turner van Straubenzee of the 17th Foot, is made up of the light companies of the 40th, 43rd, 44th, 45th, 49th, 52nd, 55th, 63rd, and 64th regiments of Foot.

August 1776: The 3rd Battalion Light Infantry is formed from the light companies of Major-General Henry Clinton's newly arrived regiments outside of New York, composed of the light-infantry companies of the 15th, 28th, 33rd, 37th, 46th, 54th, and 57th regiments of Foot.

August 6, 1776: The light company of the 42nd Regiment of Foot joins the 1st Battalion Light Infantry on Staten Island prior to the battle of Long Island on August 27.

October 23, 1776: Lieutenant-Colonel Robert Abercromby takes command of the 1st Battalion after Musgrave is injured during fighting at Throg's Neck.

March 23, 1777: The 3rd Battalion Light Infantry is disbanded and its companies split instead between the 1st and 2nd battalions. The light companies of the 15th, 28th, and 33rd regiments of Foot join the 1st Battalion while the light companies of the 37th, 46th, and 57th regiments of Foot join the 2nd Battalion. The 54th's light company joins its parent regiment on Rhode Island.

July 5, 1778: The light battalions are temporarily disbanded and their companies returned to their parent regiments.

July 31, 1778: The light battalions are re-formed.

Front view of a recreated light-infantry cap. This one, belonging to the 4th Regiment of Foot, displays features unique to the regiment, mainly the lion and number and the "crested wave" design of the front plate. Many regiments appear to have altered the style of their caps or procured unique ones, varying the shape, plumage, and the device on the front according to the taste of the regiment's colonel. (Courtesy of the 4th Regiment of Foot)

August 1778: The light company of the 37th Foot is transferred from the 2nd Battalion Light Infantry to the 1st Battalion.

October 24, 1778: The light companies of the 4th, 5th, 15th, 27th, 28th, 35th, 40th, 46th, and 49th regiments of Foot along with their parent regiments are placed under the command of Major-General James Grant for the expedition to St. Lucia.

November 3, 1778: The remaining light companies are re-formed into a single battalion under the command of Lieutenant-Colonel Robert Abercromby.

December 15, 1779: The light companies are again split into two battalions, the 1st consisting of the light companies of the 7th, 22nd, 33rd, 37th, 42nd, 54th, 63rd, 70th, and 74th regiments of Foot and the 2nd of the light companies of the 17th, 23rd, 38th, 43rd, 57th, 64th, 76th, 80th, and 84th regiments of Foot.

June 28, 1780: The light company of the 82nd Regiment of Foot joins the 1st Battalion.

BIBLIOGRAPHY

Published sources

Abbatt, William (1905). *The Magazine of History with Notes and Queries, Volume 2*. Poughkeepsie, NY: William Abbatt.

Amherst, Jeffery (1887). "Orders Given This Day By General Amherst," in *Collections of the Nova Scotia Historical Society, for the Year 1886–87, Volume V*. Halifax: Morning Herald Printing and Publishing Co., pp. 107–08.

Anbury, Thomas (1789). *Travels through the Interior Parts of America in a Series of Letters, Volume 1*. London: William Lane.

André, John, ed. Henry Cabot Lodge (1903). *André's journal: an authentic record of the movements and engagements of the British Army in America from June 1777 to November 1778 as recorded from day to day by Major John André*. Boston, MA: Bibliophile Society.

Augustus, William (1936). "Cumberland to Loudon, 2 December 1756," in Stanley Pargellis, ed., *Military affairs in North America 1748–1765: selected documents from the Cumberland Papers in Windsor Castle*. New York, NY: D. Appleton-Century Co., pp. 255–56.

Braisted, Todd W. (2015). "Light Infantry Never Surrender!" in *Journal of the American Revolution*. Available online at https://allthingsliberty.com/2015/05/light-infantry-never-surrender/

Brown, Abram English (1896). *Beneath Old Roof Trees*. Boston, MA: Lee & Shepard Publishers.

Carman, W.Y. (1984). "Banastre Tarleton and the British Legion," *Journal of the Society for Army Historical Research* 62: 127–31.

Chamberlain, Mellen (1891). *Memorial of Captain Charles Cochrane a British officer of the Revolutionary War*. Cambridge, MA: John Wilson & Son.

Clayton, Anthony (2006). *The British Officer: Leading the Army from 1660 to the Present*. London: Routledge.

Coote, Eyre, transcribed by Paul L. Pace (2011). "37th Light Infantry Company Order Book, 1778–1781." Available online at http://www.revwar75.com/library/pace/37-light-OB.pdf

Cuthbertson, Bennett (1776). *A System for the Compleat Interior Management and Œconomy of a Battalion of Infantry*. Bristol: Rouths & Nelson.

Evelyn, W. Glanville, ed. G.D. Scull (1879). *Memoir and Letters of Captain W. Glanville Evelyn of the 4th Regiment, ("King's Own,") from North America, 1774–1776*. Oxford: James Parker & Co.

Fortescue, John (1911). *A History of the British Army: Volume III*. London: MacMillan & Co. Ltd.

Gates, David (1987). *The British Light Infantry Arm, 1790–1815: Its Creation, Training, and Operational Role*. London: B.T. Batsford Ltd.

Gillespie, Alexander, ed. (1803). *An Historical Review of the Royal Marine Corps, from its Original Institution Down to the Present Era, 1803*. Birmingham: M. Swinney.

Gordon, William (1885). "Copy of the Journal Kept by Gordon," *Collections of the Nova Scotia Historical Society for the Year 1884*. Halifax: William McNab.

Hagist, Don & Goldstein, Erik (2009). "Short Land Muskets for the British Light Infantry in America," *Man at Arms Magazine*, December 2009: 19–23.

Honeyman, Robert, ed. Philip Padelford (1939). *Colonial Panorama, 1775: Dr. Robert Honeyman's Journal for March and April*. San Marino, CA: The Huntington Library.

Hunter, Martin (1894). *The Journal of Gen. Sir Martin Hunter, G.C.M.G., G.C.H.: and some letters of his wife, Lady Hunter*. Edinburgh: Edinburgh Press.

Johnston, Henry Phelps (1878). *Memoirs of the Long Island Historical Society Volume 3: The Campaign of 1776 Around New York and Brooklyn*. New York, NY: The Society.

Johnston, Henry Phelps (1881). *The Yorktown Campaign and the Surrender of Cornwallis, 1781*. New York, NY: Harper & Bros.

Kembel, Stephen (1884). "Gen. Sir William Howe's Orders," in *Collections of the New York Historical Society in the Year 1884 (Vol. 16)*. New York: The New York Historical Society.

King, Julian & George Willis (1779). "Lord Stirling," in John Almon, ed., *The Remembrancer, Or Impartial Repository of Public Events, Volume 7*. London: J. Almon, pp. 293–94.

Knox, John, ed. (1769). *An Historical Journal of the Campaigns in North-America, for the Years 1757, 1758, 1759, and 1760*. London: W. Johnston & J. Dodiley.

Lamb, Roger (1811). *Memoir of His Own Life*. Dublin: J. Jones.

Lindsay, Colin (1861). "From Lord Lindsay to Mr. Pitt. Philadelphia, October 23rd, 1777," in Georgiana Chatterton, ed., *Memorials personal and historical of Admiral Lord Gambier, G.C.B.* London: Hurst & Blackett, pp. 105–10.

Lushington, S.R., ed. (1840). *The Life and Services of General Lord Harris, G.C.B. During his Campaigns in America, the West Indies, and India*. London: John W. Parker.

Mackenzie, Roderick (1787). *Strictures on Lt. Col. Tarleton's History*. London: R. Jameson.

McGuire, Thomas J. (2000). *Battle of Paoli: The Revolutionary War "Massacre" Near Philadelphia*. Mechanicsburg, PA: Stackpole Books.

Moore, Frank (1859). *Songs and Ballads of the American Revolution*. New York, NY: D. Appleton & Co.

Moore, Frank (1863). *Diary of the American Revolution from Newspapers and Original Documents*. New York, NY: Charles Scribner.

Moorsom, William Scarth (1860). *Historical Record of the Fifty-Second Regiment (Oxfordshire Light Infantry) from the Year 1755 to the Year 1858*. London: Richard Bentley.

Nelson, Paul David (2005). *Francis Rawdon-Hastings, Marquess of Hastings: Soldier, Peer of the Realm, Governor-General of India*. Cranbury, NJ: Fairleigh Dickinson University.

Redington, Joseph & Roberts, R.A. (1899). *Calendar of Home Office Papers of the Reign of George III, 1760–1775*, Vol. 4. London: Longman.

Reed, William B., ed. (1847). *Life and Correspondence of Joseph Reed, Volume 1*. Philadelphia, PA: Lindsay & Blakiston.

Robertson, James Irvine, ed. (1948). *David Stewart of Garth: Correspondence, 1772–1829*. Edinburgh: Tuckwell Press.

Rogers, George C., ed. (1964). "Letters of Charles O'Hara to the Duke of Grafton," *The South Carolina Historical Magazine*, Vol. 65, No. 3 (July 1964): 158–89.

Simcoe, John Graves (1926). *The Life of John Graves Simcoe, First Lieutenant-Governor of the Province of Upper Canada, 1792–96*, ed. William Renwick Riddell. Toronto: McClelland & Stewart.

Simes, Thomas (1781). *The Military Guide for Young Officers, Containing a System of the Art of War*. London: J. Millan.

Spring, Matthew (2008). *With Zeal and With Bayonets Only: The British Army on Campaign in North America, 1775–1783*. Norman, OK: University of Oklahoma Press.

Stirling, Alexander (1779). "Extract of a letter from Major-General Lord Stirling, date Elizabethtown, October 21, 1778," in John Almon, ed., *The Remembrancer, Or Impartial Repository of Public Events, Volume 7*. London: J. Almon, pp. 293–94.

Stirling, Anthony, ed. (1897). *The Story of the Highland Brigade in the Crimea*. London: Remington.

Strachan, Hew (1975). *British Military Uniforms, 1768–96: The Dress of the British Army from Official Sources*. London: Arms & Armour Press.

Townshend, George (1894). "Rules and Orders for the Discipline of the Light Infantry Companies in His Majesty's Army in Ireland," in Raymond Henry Raymond Smythies, ed., *Historical Records of the 40th (2nd Somersetshire) Regiment*. Devonport: A.H. Smith.

Urban, Mark (2007). *Fusiliers: Eight Years with the Redcoats in America*. London: Faber & Faber.

Urwin, Gregory J.W. (2019). "'To bring the American Army under strict Discipline': British Army Foraging Policy in the South, 1780–81," *War in History*, Vol. 26 (1): 11.

Whinyates, F.A. (1898). *The Services of Lieut.-Colonel Francis Downman*. Woolwich: The Royal Artillery Institution.

Unpublished sources

Amherst MSS, Lord Townshend to Lord Amherst, June 17, 1775. Kent Record Office 073/21, f. I.

Amherst Papers, WO 34/119, p. 85, from Reel 93, Stanford University. Transcribed by Alexander J. Good, February 1, 2006.

Cumberland to Loudoun, October 22–December 23, 1756, LO 2065.

Howe, William. *Discipline established by Major General Howe for Light Infantry in Battalion, Sarum September 1774*, National Army Museum 6807/157/6.

Laye, Francis. "Jamaica, Long Island, 12 Decr 1778," National Army Museum 6807-154.

Sullivan, Thomas, *Journal of the operations of the American War* (1779), American Philosophical Society, Mss.973.3.Su5, p. 151.

Side view of a recreated light-infantry cap. Note the three chains, ostensibly to help protect against sword strokes. The caps were usually made of boiled leather. (Courtesy of the 4th Regiment of Foot)

INDEX

References to illustrations are shown in **bold**.
Plates are shown with page locators in brackets.